SLAVERY IN THE AMERICAS

African Americans during Reconstruction

Richard Worth

Philip Schwarz, Ph.D., *General Editor*

CHELSEA HOUSE
PUBLISHERS
An imprint of Infobase Publishing

Slavery in the Americas: *African Americans during Reconstruction*

Copyright © 2006 by Infobase Publishing

Chelsea House
An imprint of Infobase Publishing
132 West 31st Street
New York NY 10001

Library of Congress Cataloging-in-Publication Data
Worth, Richard.
    Beginning a new life : African Americans during Reconstruction / Richard Worth.
            p. cm. — (Slavery in the Americas)
    Includes bibliographical references and index.
    ISBN 0-8160-6139-4
    1. African Americans—Civil rights—Southern States—History—19th century—Juvenile literature.
    2. Reconstruction (U.S. history, 1865-1877)—Juvenile literature. 3. African Americans—History—
    1863-1877—Juvenile literature. 4. African Americans—Segregation—Southern States—History—
    19th century—Juvenile literature. 5. Southern States—Race relations—Juvenile literature. I. Title. II. Series.
    E185.2.W77 2006
    973'.0496073—dc22

                                                                                2005015720

Cover design by Smart Graphics
A Creative Media Applications Production
Interior design: Fabia Wargin & Luis Leon
Editor: Matt Levine
Copy editor: Laurie Lieb
Proofreader: Tania Bissell
Photo researcher: Jennifer Bright

Photo Credits:
The Bridgeman Art Library: title page; Getty Images pages: 5, 30, 45, 89, 93, 106; Associated Press pages: 10, 19, 23, 66; New York Public Library/Art Resources page: 15; The Granger Collection, New York pages: 17, 33, 60, 69, 71, 77, 81, 83, 84, 86, 90, 96, 106; Library of Congress pages: 35, 48, 51, 53, 55, 57, 74, 105; North Wind Picture Archives pages: 39, 95, 104; Picture History pages: 40, 47, 105; Scala/Art Resources page: 101

Printed in the United States of America

VB PKG 10 9 8 7 6 5 4 3 2 1

This book is printed on acid-free paper.

PREVIOUS PAGE:

A group of freedmen (freed slaves) discuss their political rights at a convention in Georgia in 1865.

Contents

Preface to the Series

Philip Schwarz, Ph.D., *General Editor*

In order to understand American history, it is essential to know that for nearly two centuries, Americans in the 13 colonies and then in the United States bought imported Africans and kept them and their descendants in bondage. In his second inaugural address in March 1865, President Abraham Lincoln mentioned the "250 years of unrequited toil" that slaves had endured in America. Slavery lasted so long and controlled so many people's lives that it may seem impossible to comprehend the phenomenon and to know the people involved. Yet it is extremely difficult to grasp many aspects of life in today's United States without learning about slavery's role in the lives and development of the American people.

Slavery probably existed before history began to be recorded, but the first known dates of slavery are about 1600 B.C. in Greece and as early as 2700 B.C. in Mesopotamia (present-day Iraq). Although there are institutions that resemble slavery in some modern societies, slavery in its actual sense is illegal everywhere. Yet historical slavery still affects today's free societies.

Numerous ancient and modern slave societies were based on chattel slavery—the legal ownership of human beings, not just their labor. The Bible's Old and New Testaments, as well as other ancient historical documents, describe enslaved people. Throughout history, there were slaves in African, Middle Eastern, South Asian, and East Asian societies, as well as in the Americas—and of course, there were slaves in European countries. (One origin of the word *slave* is the medieval Latin *sclavus,* which not only means "slave" but also "Slav." The Slavs were people of eastern Europe who were conquered in the 800s and often sold as slaves.)

This drawing shows slaves carrying their master in a garden in ancient Rome. Slaves were a part of many societies from ancient times until the mid-1800s.

People found as many excuses or justifications for enslaving other people as there were slaveholding societies. Members of one ethnic group claimed that cultural differences justified enslaving people of another group. People with long histories of conflict with other groups might conclude that those other people were inferior in some cultural way. Citizens of ancient Greece and Rome, among others, claimed they could hold other people in bondage because these people were "barbarians" or prisoners of war. Racism played a major part in European decisions to enslave Africans. European colonists in the Americas commonly argued that Africans and their descendants were naturally inferior to Europeans, so it was morally acceptable to enslave them.

New World slavery deeply affected both Africa and the Americas. African society changed dramatically when the Atlantic slave trade began to carry so many Africans away. Some African societies were weakened by the regular buying or kidnapping of valued community members.

Western Hemisphere societies also underwent extraordinary changes when slavery of Africans was established there. Black slavery in North America was part of society from the earliest colonial settlements until the end of the U.S. Civil War. Many people consider the sale of about 20 Africans in Jamestown, Virginia, in 1619 the beginning of African slavery in what became the United States. American Indians and, later, Africans also were enslaved in Spanish colonies such as today's Florida and California and the islands of the Caribbean.

In early to mid-17th-century colonial North America, slavery developed slowly, beginning in Maryland and Virginia and spreading to the Carolinas in the 1670s. Southern colonists originally relied on white European servants. However, many of these servants had signed contracts to work only for a certain number of years, often to pay for their passage to North America. They became free when these contracts expired. Other servants rebelled or escaped. When fewer Europeans were available as servants, the servants' prices rose. The colonists hoped to find a more easily controlled and cheaper labor supply. European slave traders captured and imported more Africans, and slave prices dropped.

Soon, American plantations became strong markets for enslaved Africans. Tobacco plantation owners in the colonies around Chesapeake Bay—Maryland, Virginia, and North Carolina—and rice growers in South Carolina pressured slave traders to supply more slaves. In time, more and more slaves were kidnapped from their homes in Africa and taken to the colonies in chains to cultivate crops on the growing number of Southern plantations. Slaves were also taken to the Northern colonies to be farm workers, household servants, and artisans. In 1790, the U.S. enslaved population was less than 700,000. By 1860, it had risen to 3,953,750.

Similar circumstances transformed the Caribbean and South American societies and economies into plantation economies. There was a high demand for sugar in Europe, so British, French, Spanish, Portuguese, and other European colonists tried to fill that need. Brazil, a Portuguese colony, also became a thriving coffee-producing region. As the sugar and coffee planters became successful, they increased the size of their plantations and therefore needed more slaves to do the work. By 1790, Brazil was the largest American colonial slave society—that is, a society whose economy and social structure were grounded in slavery. Some 1,442,800 enslaved people lived in Brazil in 1790—twice the number that lived in the United States. Brazil's slave population grew slowly, however; in 1860, it was still only about 1,715,000. However, South American slaves were forced to work extremely hard in the tropical heat. The death rate of Caribbean and South American plantation workers was much higher than that of the North American slaves. Occasionally, a North American slave owner would threaten to sell unruly slaves to the West Indies or South America. Enslaved people took the threat seriously because the West Indies' bad reputation was widespread.

It is estimated that at least 11.8 million people were captured and shipped from Africa to the Americas. Many died during the slave ship voyage across the Atlantic Ocean. About 10 million survived and were sold in the Americas from 1519 to 1867. Nearly one-third of those people went to Brazil, while only about 3.8 percent (391,000) came to North America.

If the 1619 "first Africans" were slaves—the record is not completely clear—then there was a massive increase of the enslaved North American population from 20 or so people to nearly 4 million. In 1860, known descendants of Africans, both enslaved and free, numbered approximately 4.5 million, or about 14 percent of the U.S. population.

Slaveholders thought several numbers best measured their social, political, and economic status. These were the number of human beings they owned, the money and labor value of those people, and the proportion of slaveholders' total investment in human beings. By the 1800s, Southern slaveholders usually held two-thirds of their worth in human property. The largest slave owners were normally the wealthiest people in their area. For example, one Virginian colonist, Robert "King" Carter, who died in 1733, owned 734 slaves.

Consider what it took for slavery to begin in North America and to last all the way to 1865 in the South. This historical phenomenon did not "just occur." Both slave owning and enslaved people made many decisions concerning enslavement.

Should people hold other people in lifetime bondage? Could Africans be imported without damaging American colonial societies? Should colonists give up slavery? It took many years before Americans reached consensus on these subjects. White people's consensus in the North eventually led to the outlawing of slavery there. The Southern white consensus was clearly proslavery. Enslaved peoples had to make different decisions. Should slaves resist slavery individually or in groups? Should they raise families when their children were likely to live and die in bondage? Over the two centuries in which North American slavery existed, enslaved people changed their opinions concerning these questions.

Some white colonists initially tried to own Indian slaves. However, because the Indians knew the local environment, they could escape somewhat easily, especially because their free relatives and friends would try to protect them. Also, European diseases simply killed many of these Indians. Once European enslavement of American Indians died out in the 18th century, Africans and their African-American descendants were the only slaves in America. The Africans and their children were people with a history. They represented numerous African societies from West Africa to Madagascar in the western Indian Ocean. They endured and survived, creating their own American history.

When Africans began families in North America, they created a new genealogy and new traditions regarding how to survive as slaves. They agonized over such matters as violent, or even group, resistance—if it was unlikely to succeed, why try? By the 1800s, they endured family losses to the interstate slave trade. Black families suffered new separations that often were as wrenching as those caused by the journey from Africa. Large numbers of black Americans were forced to move from the older (Upper South) states to the newer (Deep South) territories and states. They were often ripped from their families and everything they knew and forced to live and work in faraway places.

This undated illustration of pre–Civil War life depicts African men being held in slave pens in Washington, D.C., about 1850.

There was only so much that African-American people could do to resist enslavement once it became well established in America. People sometimes ask why slaves did not try to end their bondage by revolting. Some did, but they rarely succeeded in freeing themselves. Most individual "revolts"—more accurately termed resistance—were very localized and were more likely to succeed than large-scale revolts. A man or woman might refuse to do what owners wanted, take the punishment, and find another way to resist. Some were so effective in day-to-day resistance that they can be called successful. Others failed and then decided that they had to try to find ways to survive slavery and enjoy some aspects of life. Those who escaped as "fugitives," temporarily or permanently, were the most successful resisters. Frederick Douglass and Harriet Tubman are the most famous escapees. Solomon Northup was unique: He was born free, then kidnapped and sold into slavery. Northup escaped and published his story.

Although inhumane and designed to benefit slave owners, slavery was a very "human" institution. That is, slaveholders and enslaved people interacted in many different ways. The stories of individuals reveal this frequently complex human interaction.

There were, for example, in all the Southern states, free African Americans who became slave owners. They protected their own family members from slavery, but owned other human beings for profit. One such black slave owner, William Johnson of Mississippi, controlled his human property using the same techniques, both mild and harsh, as did white slave owners. Robert Lumpkin, a slave trader from Richmond, Virginia, sold thousands of human beings to

Deep South buyers. Yet Lumpkin had a formerly enslaved wife to whom he willed all his Virginia, Alabama, and Pennsylvania property in 1866. Lumpkin sent their children to Massachusetts and Pennsylvania for their education and protection. He also freed other slaves before 1865. How could men such as these justify protecting their own families, but at the same time separating so many other families?

The Thirteenth Amendment ended slavery in the United States. However, former slaves were often kept from owning property and did not share the same rights as white Americans. Racist laws and practices kept the status of black Americans low. Even though slavery ended well over a century ago, the descendants of slave owners and of slaves are still generally on markedly different economic levels from each other.

The Civil War and Reconstruction created massive upheaval in Southern slave and free black communities. In addition, slave owners were often devastated. African Americans were "free at last," but their freedom was not guaranteed. A century passed before their legal rights were effectively protected and their political participation expanded. The Reverend Martin Luther King's "I have a dream" speech placed the struggle in historical context: He said he had a dream that "the sons of former slaves and the sons of former slave owners will be able to sit down together at the table of brotherhood." (Today, he would surely mention daughters as well.) The weight of history had already delayed that dream's coming to pass and can still do so. Knowing the history of slavery and emancipation will help fulfill the dream.

Introduction

The Emancipation Proclamation of 1863 freed the slaves. However, the Reconstruction period following the Civil War from 1865 to 1877 was filled with turmoil for these newly freed Americans.

Slaves were first brought from Africa to the Americas during the early 16th century. The Spanish conquistadores, who had established colonies on the Caribbean islands and in Central America, wanted slaves to work their sugar plantations. The Dutch and English also established colonies in the Americas, and their traders began transporting slaves from Africa.

In 1619, a Dutch trader brought a shipload of Africans to Virginia, an English colony in North America. During the 17th century, slaves worked on the tobacco plantations in Virginia and Maryland and on the rice plantations in the Carolinas. Southern colonies established strict laws to control the slaves. These laws prevented slaves from leaving their plantations without passes. Slave owners were permitted to whip their slaves brutally without being punished by the law. Slaves who ran away from their masters could be executed.

By the beginning of the 18th century, the slave population had grown to about 23,000 in the South. About 5,000 slaves also lived in the North, working on farms and as artisans in towns. Over the next century, the slave population expanded greatly. More slaves were imported from Africa. In addition, the slaves themselves produced families. By the early 19th century, the slave population in the South had exploded to over 1 million. In the North, by contrast, slavery was gradually abolished, or forbidden, following the American Revolution (1775–1783).

Slavery continued to grow in the South over the next half-century. Meanwhile, the value of a slave rose higher and higher, more than tripling between 1800 and 1860. Adult slaves were valued at $1,000 to $1,500. This was a large amount of money at that time, equivalent to approximately $32,000 today.

The 4 million slaves living in Southern states in 1860 made up about one-third of the total population of these states. In addition, there were about 500,000 free blacks living in the United States in 1860. About half of them lived in the South and half in the North.

In 1860, there were 4 million African-American slaves. Slavery lay at the heart of the South's economy. Slaves worked on the profitable sugar, tobacco, rice, and cotton plantations that stretched across the South. They were expected to work long days in the fields and were routinely beaten if they refused to obey their masters.

Plantation owners measured their wealth not only in terms of cotton or sugar but by the number of slaves they owned. Slave owners who needed extra money thought nothing of selling off individual members of slave families, including children. An estimated 20 to 30 percent of slave families were broken apart through sales. Although some slaves tried to avoid their harsh fate by running away and escaping to the North, most remained on the plantations.

Slavery thrived in the South. Plantation owners also wanted to expand the institution of slavery westward. However, slavery came under attack from Northerners. Northern abolitionists—people who wanted to end slavery—spoke out against the institution in the press, while Northern political leaders denounced slavery in Congress.

In this lithograph from the mid-1800s, slaves harvest cotton in the fields of a Mississippi plantation while the plantation owners look on.

Throughout much of Latin America, slavery had been abolished by 1860. That year, voters in the United States elected Abraham Lincoln as president. The first Republican president, Lincoln was committed to ending the expansion of slavery. Shortly after his election, Southern states began to leave the Union. Many Southerners feared that Lincoln threatened the future of slavery. As Lincoln himself had stated before his election, "A House divided against itself cannot stand. I believe this government cannot endure, permanently half slave and half free."

The Southern states established a new government, the Confederate States of America. The capital was first located in Montgomery, Alabama, and later moved to Richmond, Virginia. Still, President Lincoln hoped to avoid a civil war. In his first inaugural address, delivered in March 1861, Lincoln said: "We are not enemies, but friends. We must not be enemies. Though passion may have strained, it must not break our bonds of affection."

In April, however, Confederate forces fired on Fort Sumter—the Union fortress in the harbor of Charleston, South Carolina. Civil war swept across America for the next four years.

1

Lincoln and Reconstruction

This American cartoon, from around the time of the presidential campaign of 1864, shows the "Rail Splitter" Abraham Lincoln and his running mate, Andrew Johnson, the Tennessee tailor, and points out the task of Reconstruction that lay ahead of them.

PRESIDENT LINCOLN'S VIEWS OF SLAVERY

On January 1, 1863, President Abraham Lincoln issued the Emancipation Proclamation. In this official public announcement, President Lincoln *stated that "all persons held as slaves* within any State . . . in rebellion against the United States, shall be . . . thenceforward, and forever free."

Eleven months later, the president proclaimed his first Reconstruction plan. This plan was designed to rebuild, or reconstruct, the Union after the Civil War (1861–1865). The plan detailed a way that the Southern states fighting against the North could once again become part of the Union. The Reconstruction plan called on Southern states to swear their loyalty to the Union and free their slaves. Lincoln thus laid the foundation for Reconstruction, which did not really begin until the Civil War had ended. Lasting from 1865 until 1877, the Reconstruction era dealt with two key issues: how the Southern states would be readmitted to the Union and how the former African-American slaves would be treated—that is, whether they would receive the same rights as white citizens.

At first, Lincoln's main focus was to win the war and put the Union back together. However, Lincoln gradually became interested in abolishing slavery as a means of defeating the South.

Lincoln told newspaper editor Horace Greeley in 1862, "My paramount object in this struggle is to save the Union, and is not either to save or to destroy slavery. If I could save the Union without freeing any slave I would do it." Lincoln feared that by freeing the slaves, he would only anger the "border states," which might then join the Confederacy. In these states—Maryland, Delaware, Missouri, and Kentucky—many people owned slaves. The border states mostly supported the South, and some of their residents even joined the Confederate army.

By the President of the United States of America:

A. Proclamation.

Whereas, on the twenty-second day of September, in the year of our Lord one thousand eight hundred and sixty-two, a proclamation was issued by the President of the United States, containing, among other things, the following, to wit:

"That on the first day of January, in the

This image from the National Archives shows the first page of the original Emancipation Proclamation. The poor quality of the paper and ink make it vulnerable to light, so it is only occasionally brought out of storage.

During 1862, however, the focus of the Union war effort began to change. President Lincoln was looking for a way to undermine the Confederate war effort. With slaves working on the plantations and in Southern factories, most white Southerners were freed up to join the Confederate armies. As a result, these armies could hold their own against Northern forces in the field. However, if the slaves were freed, they would no longer play a vital role in the Southern economy. Many of them, Lincoln believed, would escape from their masters and work for the Union cause. Freed slaves might also bring more troops into the Union army, greatly strengthening the Union war effort.

In 1862, Congress passed the Militia Act. This law gave Lincoln the power to raise 300,000 militiamen to fight in the Union army. The president was also permitted to grant freedom to any of the militia who were slaves.

Later that year, Lincoln discussed with the members of his cabinet a proclamation freeing the slaves. The president explained his reasons for issuing such a proclamation. However, he wanted to time the proclamation with a Union victory. In September 1862, Union forces beat back Confederate general Robert E. Lee's invasion of Maryland at the Battle of Antietam. Lincoln had the victory he needed. Soon afterward, he issued the Emancipation Proclamation. This act freed the slaves only in those states that belonged to the Confederacy, not the border states.

As Union troops invaded the South, they took over Southern territory. They now had the power to free all the slaves there. Many African Americans did not wait for the Union armies. As one former slave, Mary Crane, recalled, "When President Lincoln issued his Proclamation, freeing the Negroes, I remember that my father and most all of the other younger slave men left the farms."

Many plantation owners did not tell their slaves about the Emancipation Proclamation. Most White Southerners had no intention of doing what the proclamation demanded. However, some slaves heard about the proclamation from other white Southerners who believed in emancipation.

In addition, many slaves were told about emancipation by a group of black agents sent across the South by the Union leaders. As one of these agents, George Washington Albright, recalled, "I traveled about the plantations within a certain range, and got together small meetings in the cabins to tell the slaves the great news. Some of these slaves in turn would find their way to still other plantations—and so the story spread. We had to work in dead secrecy." If Albright had been caught by Confederate officials, he would have been executed. Also, the slaves who met with Albright traveled from plantation to plantation without permission from their white masters. If the slaves had been captured, they would have been severely punished—perhaps even hanged.

THE BEGINNING OF RECONSTRUCTION

In 1863, the tide of the war turned against the South. Southern armies lost the decisive battle at Gettysburg, Pennsylvania, in July. At the same time, Northern armies captured the Confederate stronghold at Vicksburg, Mississippi, on the Mississippi River.

In December 1863, President Lincoln issued his first Proclamation of Amnesty and Reconstruction. It was called the Ten Percent Plan. The plan stated that Southern states could reenter the Union if 10 percent of their population took a loyalty oath to the U.S. government. Each state must also agree to outlaw slavery. Lincoln's Reconstruction plan was very easy on the South. His major goal was to end the Civil War as quickly as possible and bring Southerners back into the Union. He wanted to avoid hard feelings, so the North and the South could rapidly work together again.

The Southern armies did not stop fighting, however. During 1864, some of the war's bloodiest battles occurred. Union forces approached Richmond and captured Atlanta, Georgia. The success of Lincoln's armies ensured that the president would be reelected in 1864. Meanwhile, Congress was considering the Thirteenth Amendment to the Constitution. This amendment called for an end to slavery in the United States. The amendment was passed by Congress on January 31, 1865, and later approved by the states.

During 1865, President Lincoln began to plan for the end of the war and Reconstruction. He modified his Ten Percent Plan to require that all Southern states approve the Thirteenth Amendment. Lincoln also talked about giving the right to vote to some African Americans. Lincoln believed that only some former slaves should be permitted to vote. He said, "I would myself prefer that [the vote] were now conferred on the very intelligent, and on those who serve our cause as soldiers." Many Republicans agreed that freedom meant more than just breaking the chains of slavery. It also meant the right to vote, hold elected office, and own property. As one Northern Republican, Congressman James A. Garfield, put it, "What is freedom? Is it the bare privilege of not being chained? . . . If this is all, then freedom is a bitter mockery."

In March 1865, Lincoln delivered his second inaugural address. "With malice toward none; with charity for all," Lincoln said, "with firmness in the right, as God gives us to see the right, let us strive on, to finish the work we are in; to bind up the nation's wounds. . . ." He hoped to bring the Union back together as quickly and easily as possible during Reconstruction. On April 9, 1865, shortly after the president delivered these words, Confederate forces surrendered to the Union at Appomattox Courthouse in Virginia.

This painting shows the second inauguration of Abraham Lincoln as he takes the oath of office as the 16th president of the United States in front of the U.S. Capitol in Washington, D.C., on March 4, 1865. The oath was administered by Chief Justice Salmon P. Chase.

During the 1820s, most Spanish colonies in Latin America achieved their independence in bloody wars against Spain. Many of the new countries immediately abolished slavery. In Venezuela, full emancipation did not occur right away. African Americans in Venezuela who had joined the war against Spain were immediately freed. The children of slaves were emancipated. However, all their parents were not freed until 1854. In Argentina, full emancipation of the slaves did not occur until 1861.

Brazil—a Portuguese colony—continued to practice slavery. Brazil achieved its independence in the 1820s, under the leadership of Emperor Dom Pedro I. His son, Dom Pedro II, freed some of his own slaves by 1864. The children of Brazilian slaves were gradually freed during the 1870s. However, only 12,000 slaves—a small percentage of the total slave population—had been freed by 1883. Five years later, Brazil passed a law freeing all slaves.

Slaves in the Caribbean were gradually freed by England, France, Spain, and the Netherlands. All of these nations had established colonies in the Caribbean. The last colonies to abolish slavery were Puerto Rico in 1873 and Cuba in 1886.

The war had been very costly for the South. In four years 135,000 men had been killed or wounded—more than 10 percent of all Confederate soldiers. The economic destruction was crushing, estimated at $1.5 billion—equivalent to about $9 billion today. Many cities and towns, including Richmond, Virginia, the Confederate capital, had been completely destroyed. Many Southern plantations had been occupied by invading Northern armies and their cotton fields were ruined. Also, the South no longer had slaves to work in the fields. In short, the way of life that the South had known for more than two centuries had ended. As a result, many white Southerners hated the North, which had destroyed their culture and society.

By contrast, at the end of the war, African Americans celebrated their freedom. As former slave Houston Holloway recalled, "I felt like a bird out of a cage. Amen. Amen. Amen. I could hardly ask to feel any better than I did that day. . . . The week passed off in a blaze of glory." Huge celebrations among African Americans broke out in Charleston, South Carolina, and in other parts of the South. Many former slaves sang the praises of President Lincoln for his role in ending slavery. As former slave Lewis Jenkins put it, "I think Abe Lincoln was next to Jesus Christ. The best human man ever lived."

THE NEW TASTE OF FREEDOM

Early in April 1865, after the Confederacy surrendered, President Lincoln visited the Confederate capital, Richmond, where he was hailed by the city's African-American population. He then returned to Washington, D.C., to begin rebuilding the nation after the war.

On April 14, to the horror of much of the American nation, Lincoln was assassinated. The assassin was an actor and Confederate sympathizer named John Wilkes Booth. Two weeks later, Booth was hunted down and killed.

African Americans by the thousands participated in funeral services for the president. Meanwhile, Southern soldiers were returning to their plantations after the war. Some of them began giving orders to African Americans and treating them as slaves. These Southerners wanted to restore conditions that had existed before the Civil War. "I saw white men whipping colored [African-American] men just the same as they did before the war," former slave Henry Adams said. But many African Americans had no intention of putting up with such treatment. Now that they were free, they intended to enjoy their freedom.

The former slaves could now go and live where they liked. Thousands left the plantations and headed for Southern cities, such as Charleston, Richmond, and Memphis, Tennessee, hoping to begin new lives. In some cities like Charleston, blacks became a majority of the population. As a result of former slaves leaving plantations in the 1860s, the black population in Southern cities grew by 75 percent.

Some masters seemed genuinely shocked that their former slaves wanted to leave.

The Freedmen's Bureau

Following emancipation, African Americans were often assisted in their searches for family members by the newly established Freedmen's Bureau. Congress created the Freedmen's Bureau on March 3, 1865. The agency was directed by General Oliver O. Howard, a Civil War hero committed to emancipation. Howard said early in the Civil War, "God means us to free all the slaves." Howard and his assistants handled several types of work in the South. Their work included providing food and clothing for poor African Americans, handling legal cases between whites and blacks, and enabling former slaves to receive an education. The bureau also helped reunite African-American families that had been separated by slavery.

They expected more loyalty from the African Americans. Those masters who had been kind to their slaves and not whipped them were especially upset. But as one former slave told her master, "I must go. If I stays here I'll never know I'm free."

As the former slaves left the plantations, they also changed their lifestyles. Throughout the era of slavery, African-American women had been forced to dress modestly. Most were given simple gray clothing to wear in the fields or in their masters' houses. Once freedom arrived, many African-American women dressed in more colorful clothing. They wore ribbons and fancy hats that were often purchased for them by their husbands. These men were proud to see their wives so well dressed and felt proud of being able to afford fancy clothes.

During slavery, about one-quarter of African-American families in the South had been cruelly broken apart by their masters. The white plantation owners sold off mothers or fathers, separating them from their families. After the war, African Americans began searching for lost family members who had been sold to other plantations. They placed advertisements in local newspapers. One ad in Nashville, Tennessee, read: "During the year 1849, Thomas Sample carried away from this city, as his slaves, our daughter, Polly and son. . . . We will give $100 each for them to any person who will assist them . . . to get to Nashville, or get word to us of their whereabouts." Some of the advertisements were successful. One former slave, Laura Redmoun, found her mother "and she came to live with me." Another former slave, Kate Drumgold, was reunited with her children.

EDUCATION AND RELIGION

During the more than two centuries of slavery, a majority of African-American slaves had not been permitted by their masters to learn to read or write. White slave owners feared that literate slaves might communicate with each other and join together to start a rebellion. After the Civil War ended, African Americans were eager to get an education. Many schools were established with aid from the Freedmen's Bureau. Northern teachers, many of them young women, came south to instruct African-American children and adults. Blacks also established their own schools. Over the next five years, they spent over $1 million to build schools.

During the 19th century, Wallace Turnage kept a diary of his experiences during slavery. He had been taught to read and write by his mother. While he was a slave, Turnage witnessed members of African-American families being sold off.

. . . one morning, a number of "Plantation Hands," formed into long line, with little Bundles [strapped] to their backs . . . all marched off to be Sold South away from all that was near and dear to them. . . . wives husbands and children; all separated one from another perhaps never to meet again on earth. I shall never forget the weeping . . . among those that were left . . . each one expecting to go next.

In 1864, Turnage escaped and found safety among Union forces.

Many schools were set up in local churches. During the slave era, African Americans had often been forced to attend churches run by whites. They were required to sit in the back or outside and listen to white ministers preach about obeying white masters. Some slaves, however, had refused to attend white churches. Instead, they held secret church gatherings in the woods near their plantations. These church gatherings were sometimes discovered by white slave patrols. The patrols traveled the roadways stopping slaves without passes or arresting groups of slaves who were meeting together. A sentry was often posted outside a church gathering to warn the other slaves when a patrol was approaching. The blacks quickly broke up their meeting before being discovered.

After the Civil War, African Americans started their own churches. Many church groups were very poor and had to hold services in rundown sheds or in families' homes. Others pooled what little money they had to buy land and erect their own church buildings. In Charleston, blacks built Emanuel Church, which cost $10,000. Some contributed money, and those who had none helped construct the church building. Many white Southerners wanted African Americans to have separate churches. Some well-to-do whites even gave African Americans land for a church and helped them put up a building.

Thousands of African Americans joined the Baptist Church or the African Methodist Episcopal Church. On Sundays, these church services were attended by large congregations. Describing one of these congregations, a newspaper reporter wrote, "Overflowing all the church-yard, flooding the road, through which . . . carriages could hardly be driven and backing up against the graveyard, were the Negroes, gay with holiday attire [clothes]." Services were held not only on Sundays but also during the week. Often, these services began early in the morning with prayers and hymns. During the services, African Americans recalled their lack of freedom during slavery, the importance of emancipation, and their desire to remain free in the future.

African-American Marriages

During the era of slavery, African-American marriages were not recognized by state laws in the South. Many couples wed each other in simple ceremonies. Some of them simply jumped over a broomstick in front of their friends, which made their marriage official, and these couples often lived together for many years. After the Civil War ended, African-American couples wanted to legalize their marriages. The Freedmen's Bureau issued marriage licenses to them. One couple, Smart and Mary Washington, formalized a marriage that had lasted for over 40 years. According to one observer, "They were very happy when they walked away together side by side, for the first time endowed with the honorable title of husband and wife."

This painting from about 1820 shows a slave wedding ceremony. Since slaves were not allowed to legally marry, the ceremonies were often held in secret and mixed traditions from African, Caribbean, and Christian religions.

Churches not only held religious services, they were also the centers of social life in black communities. They put on plays, held picnics, and organized parades. In addition, African-American churches established self-help societies. These were frequently run by women. They held dances and fairs to raise money to provide financial aid to the poor. The societies provided food, clothing, wood to heat homes, and help to former slaves who were looking for jobs. Many self-help societies were also concerned about caring for orphans. During slavery, many small children had been sold by their masters and separated from their families. After the children were freed at the end of the Civil War, they left the plantations. There was often no one to care for these orphans until the self-help societies stepped in and provided them with new homes.

As historian Eric Foner has written, "Reconstruction witnessed the birth of the modern black community." This community was based on the church, the family, the schools, and the self-help societies.

THE DESIRE FOR LAND

Most African Americans believed that freedom could not be permanent unless they also had financial security. The best way to achieve this security, they felt, was by owning land. Many thought that they should be given some of the property that made up the plantations. After all, African Americans said, they had worked hard to make the plantations economically successful, so they should get some benefit from them. As one former slave said, "Our wives, our children, our husbands, has been sold over and over again to purchase the lands we now locates on . . . we has a right to [that] land . . . didn't we clear the land and raise de crops. . . . And den didn't dem large cities in de North grow up on de cotton and de sugars and de rice dat we made?" A few blacks occupied the plantations of their former masters and started to farm the land on their own.

In 1865, Congress set up the National Freedmen's Savings and Trust Company. Many African Americans put their savings into the bank, which opened local offices across the South. Some black farmers joined together to raise as much as $5,000 to buy land. White Southerners refused to sell any land to African Americans, however, afraid that they might become too successful. (A few landowners did give their former slaves small land holdings.) Meanwhile, the Freedmen's Bureau received letters from African Americans asking for land. The Freedmen's Bureau itself held about 850,000 acres (344,000 ha) of land that had been taken from rebellious Southerners during the war. Some members of the bureau wanted African Americans to receive this land to start their own farms.

The new president, Andrew Johnson, disagreed. After Lincoln's assassination, Vice President Johnson had become president of the United States. Former slaves wanted to increase their newfound freedom, but President Johnson, a Southerner, tried in some ways to roll back the clock to the days when whites in the South controlled the lives of blacks. As a result, conflict broke out over Reconstruction.

2

The Early Days of Reconstruction

Freedmen are shown registering to vote in 1870 in the first municipal
election in Richmond, Virginia, held after the end of the Civil War.

ANDREW JOHNSON

Much like Abraham Lincoln, President Andrew Johnson presented a Reconstruction plan that was easy on the South. Many white Southerners nevertheless decided that they would return to the past. Southern states passed a series of Black Codes that denied African Americans equal rights.

Like Lincoln, President Johnson believed that the Southern states should be admitted back into the Union quickly and easily. He did not think that Southern society should be forced to make any major changes or that the federal government should tell Southerners how to run their states. He did not believe that African Americans should be given land taken from white plantation owners. Nor did he believe that former slaves should have the right to vote. Johnson feared that voting rights would give African Americans too much power. "White men alone must manage the South," he said. Johnson believed that African Americans had less "capacity for government than any other race of people. . . . Wherever they have been left to their own devices," he added, "they have shown a constant tendency to relapse into barbarism."

PRESIDENT JOHNSON'S PLAN

President Johnson planned to keep whites in power in the South. Under his Reconstruction plan, most people who had served in the Confederate army received pardons. This meant that all their property—except slaves—that was taken by Union soldiers during the Civil War was given back to them.

President Johnson also permitted Southerners to form state militias. These were groups of white men, armed with weapons, who were supposed to protect other Southerners. They were similar to the slave patrols that had existed before the Civil War. These earlier patrols had terrorized the slaves.

Johnson also appointed governors in the Southern states. These men were often sympathetic to whites and made certain that African Americans would not receive the right to vote. The governors ran the state governments until conventions could be held. Johnson allowed former members of the Confederate army to vote for delegates to these conventions. At the con-

This extract from the 1868 constitution of the state of Louisiana shows portraits of Lieutenant Governor Oscar J. Dunn, seated at his desk, and 29 African-American delegates to the Louisiana Constitutional Convention.

ventions, Southerners were expected to write new state constitutions. These constitutions were required to prohibit slavery and approve the Thirteenth Amendment. Under the new constitutions, white Southerners could be nominated to run for the state legislature, governor, and Congress. Afterward, the Southern states were to be readmitted to the Union.

While white Southerners were getting ready for their conventions, African Americans were holding their own conventions in cities across the South. These meetings were led by black men who had been free before the Civil War. Most were former slaves who had saved enough money to purchase freedom from their masters. These African Americans knew how to read and write. Many were teachers or ministers. Among the people attending these conventions were many former slaves, who had been selected as delegates by their churches. Many of these delegates were poor farmers, shabbily dressed, yet eager to preserve the freedom that they had achieved as a result of the Civil War.

African Americans had decided to hold these conventions to make sure that their needs were heard by the government in Washington. At the South Carolina convention, delegates said that they were asking "only for *even-handed Justice*. We simply desire that we shall be recognized as men, that the same laws which govern white men shall direct colored men . . . that we be dealt with as others, in equity and justice."

WHITE ATTITUDES TOWARD AFRICAN AMERICANS

Most white Southerners believed that society should remain much as it was in the days before the Civil War. One Southerner said that "the old relation of master and slave . . . had received the divine sanction [approval of God] and was the best condition in which the two races could live together for mutual benefit."

Even after the slaves had been freed, whites were still prejudiced against them. They did not consider blacks to be the equal of whites. Carl Schurz, a politician and a major general in the Union army during the Civil War, traveled to the South during Reconstruction. He wrote:

> wherever I go—the street, the shop, the house, the hotel, or the steamboat—I hear the people talk in such a way as to indicate that they are unable to [conceive] of the Negro as possessing any rights at all. Men who are honorable in their dealings with their white neighbors, will cheat a Negro without feeling a single twinge. . . . To kill a Negro, they do not deem [believe it to be] murder . . . to take the property away from a Negro, they do not consider robbery.

Although African Americans had become free, whites still believed that they should control the lives of black people. For example, many whites believed that they should be able to whip African Americans who worked for them. As a member of the Freedmen's Bureau explained, most whites believed that it was acceptable, "if a Negro says anything or does anything that they don't like, to take a gun and put a bullet into him, or a charge of shot [from a shotgun]." In addition, blacks were hanged and tortured. Some black men who were suspected of threatening white women, even though there was no evidence of their guilt, became the targets of vigilantes who beat and killed them. These vigilantes were former Confederate soldiers who rode across the Southern countryside, often attacking African-American homes at night and terrorizing black families.

AN AFRICAN-AMERICAN REVOLT

Many white Southerners feared that the free African Americans might start a revolution. Slave revolts had occurred several times in the past. Before the Civil War, slaves were given a holiday at Christmas and New Year's.

This was a time when whites were especially afraid that African Americans might escape from their plantations and begin a revolt. Such fear arose before Christmas 1865. This was known as the "Christmas Insurrection Scare of 1865."

Some African Americans believed that Christmas 1865 might be an important time for them, too. Historians are convinced that black people

Slave uprisings occurred in South Carolina in 1739. Another attempted revolt was uncovered by whites in Charleston in 1821. In 1831, slaves rose up in Virginia, led by Nat Turner. They killed more than 50 whites before the revolt was put down, and Turner was hanged.

were not planning a revolt. Nor did any revolt occur. However, African Americans were hoping that perhaps the federal government might do something special for them.

One African American, Sam McAllum from Mississippi, recalled that he heard a "heap of talk" about every black man being given "forty acres [16 ha] and a mule." There were rumors in the African-American community that Congress would give land to the freed slaves. As a result, their expectations were very high. African Americans had long hoped to own land, and some believed that their wishes might soon be fulfilled. In fact, some members of Congress had talked about giving land to African Americans so they could start their own farms. "I don't know how us come to hear about it," McAllum added. "It just kind of got around. I picked out my mule. All of us did."

Indeed, the Freedmen's Bureau had taken over almost 1 million acres (405,000 ha) of land from Southerners—but the Johnson administration did not intend to give it to African Americans. Instead, President Johnson had decided to stay out of the South's affairs. He preferred to let the Southern states themselves handle the future of African Americans.

This map of the United States from 1861 shows the Southern states that seceded from the Union and were subject to Reconstruction following the Civil War.

BLACK CODES

As time went on, President Johnson began to think that some African Americans should be permitted to vote. As he wrote to the governor of Mississippi, if the vote could be given to

all persons of color who can read the Constitution of the United States in English and write their names, and to all persons of color who own real estate valued at not less than two hundred and forty dollars . . . you would . . . set an example the other states will follow.

Former slaves are shown on their way to Kansas in this photograph from the 1870s. They are fleeing from the Black Codes and sharecrop labor of the post–Civil War South.

However, Mississippi and the other Southern states ignored President Johnson. In each state only white voters elected representatives to the U.S. Congress and the new state legislatures.

The new state legislatures were run by white men who were prejudiced against African Americans. In each state they passed laws called Black Codes. The purpose of the codes was to keep African Americans in an unequal position throughout the South.

Historian Page Smith explains that the whites in the South were afraid of African Americans for several reasons. They feared that former slaves would rise up and attack their former masters. Therefore, the Black Codes prevented African Americans from owning guns, ammunition, or knives. Whites were also afraid that blacks would not go back to work on the plantations unless they were forced to work there. As a result, white planters might not be able to make a living. Therefore, the Black Codes required African Americans to work on the plantations.

Liberia

One way for African Americans to deal with racial prejudice was to leave the United States. In 1821, the colony of Liberia was established on the west coast of Africa. As a colony of the United States, Liberia was set up as a refuge for free African Americans. About 15,000 African Americans went to Liberia over the next decades.

Liberia became an independent nation in 1847. In 1865, 346 blacks from the Caribbean island of Barbados immigrated to Liberia. After the Civil War, some African Americans also went there from the United States. In 1878, for example, 200 African Americans went to Liberia from Charleston.

In fact, the most severe Black Codes had to do with work. In Mississippi, for example, each African American adult had to prove that he or she had a job at the start of each year. This usually meant employment on a plantation. Any workers who left their jobs on plantations before the end of the year lost all their wages. Anyone who did not have a job—a person known as a vagrant—could be sent to jail or forced to pay a fine.

On the plantations, white owners paid blacks who still worked there as little as possible. Some blacks received standing wages. This meant they were paid in cash at the end of the year. Those who did not remain that long were paid nothing. Other workers received a share of the crop. This share was split between gangs of workers, each of which might receive only an eighth or a twelfth of the crop.

In addition to the laws about vagrants, the codes included an apprenticeship law. This law reduced the freedom of African-American families. Some Southern children were orphans because their parents had died during the Civil War. These children were often raised by relatives. However, the Black Codes permitted Southern courts to force African-American orphans to work as apprentices for white plantation owners without being paid. In fact, any other black children who the court decided were not being properly raised by their parents could be taken from the parents and forced to work for free. Before emancipation, children were regularly sold away from their parents. Whites used the apprenticeship laws to treat these children as orphans and prevent them from enjoying the freedom granted under the Thirteenth Amendment.

Some African-American parents wrote to the Freedmen's Bureau asking for help. Others decided to act on their own. One of these was Jane Kamper, whose children were being forced to serve as apprentices. As she told the Freedmen's Bureau, William Townsend "locked my children up so that I could not find them. I afterwards got my children by stealth [stole them] and brought them to Baltimore." Kamper left home so quickly that she could not take her furniture. She asked the Freedmen's Bureau to help her recover it.

The Black Codes separated whites and blacks. Segregation, as this separation was called, continued during much of the 20th century. In Texas, for example, African Americans were forced to sit in separate railroad cars after the Civil War. South Carolina prevented African Americans from doing any kind of work except farming without special permission from the courts. In other states, African Americans could not sit in parks with whites.

In some cities, however, segregation rules were overturned. In 1866, African Americans protested segregation on streetcars in Louisiana's capital, New Orleans. As a result, a federal military commander who still had troops there after the Civil War ordered that segregation must be ended. Similar protests occurred in Charleston and Richmond, where segregation on streetcars was also ended.

White militias patrolled the countryside. The patrols picked up people thought to be vagrants. They also broke into the homes of African Americans, looking for weapons. In Florida, any African American caught with a weapon could receive 39 lashes with a whip.

Nevertheless, African Americans did receive a few rights. In the Southern states, African Americans could own property if any white Southerners were willing to sell it to them. African Americans could also serve on juries in courts, but they could not go to court and give evidence against white Southerners. One observer noted that this meant "the verdicts are always for the white man against the colored man."

The Freedmen's Bureau tried to step in and help African Americans. It set up courts to try some cases involving African Americans. The bureau also tried to make sure that black laborers were fairly paid for their work—a wage of eight to 10 dollars monthly. However, the bureau was unable to do much more. White prejudice against African Americans had begun hundreds of years earlier. This prejudice would not just disappear in a few years as a result of the Civil War.

In addition, the white majority controlled the local government and most of the courts. African Americans had very little money to pay lawyers to represent them in trials. As a result, blacks could not receive justice against whites who abused them. Without the right to vote, blacks could do little to change the government and improve their situation. However, the conditions in the South were about to change.

3

A New Reconstruction Plan

This collage of photographs shows black and white radical members of
South Carolina's first Reconstruction legislature in 1870.

THE RADICAL REPUBLICANS

President Johnson wanted the Southern states back in the Union, and he was prepared to take them back even with the Black Codes. Throughout the North, there were different opinions about Johnson's Reconstruction policies. Some people supported the president, hoping that the cotton plantations would be running as soon as possible. Clothing manufacturers, for example, needed cotton to make a profit in their mills. However, other members of Johnson's Republican Party opposed him. Called the Radical Republicans, they believed that the Black Codes might undo much that the Civil War had been fought to accomplish.

These Radical Republicans were led by Senator Charles Sumner of Massachusetts and Congressman Thaddeus Stevens of Pennsylvania. Sumner and Stevens wanted to give emancipated black men voting rights. The law applied only to males, because no women of any race would be able to vote until 1920. As Stevens told Congress early in 1867, the right to vote for blacks might mean that

> loyal governments may be established in most of those [Southern] States. Without it all are sure to be ruled by traitors; and loyal men, black and white will be oppressed, exiled or murdered. . . . Have not loyal blacks quite as good a right to choose rulers and make laws as rebel whites?

Stevens also believed that African Americans should be given their own land.

This 1866 campaign poster attacks James Geary, a Radical Republican supporter of African-American suffrage in Pennsylvania, and supports Democrat Hiester Clymer's campaign for governor. Geary won the election.

THE MODERATE REPUBLICANS

The Radical Republicans wanted to make major changes in the South. However, the majority of Republicans disagreed. These moderate Republicans supported some rights for African Americans. In 1866, the moderate Republicans proposed a civil rights bill in Congress. This stated that every American citizen should have the same rights, such as the right to own property, but the bill did not include the right to vote. Another bill proposed that the Freedmen's Bureau should continue to serve the needs of former slaves in the South. A majority of Congress passed both these bills.

However, President Johnson vetoed them. He believed that the federal government did not have the power to force states to guarantee equal rights for their citizens.

Charles Sumner

Born in Boston, Massachusetts, in 1811, Charles Sumner later attended Harvard University and then became a lawyer. During the 1840s, Sumner opposed segregation in Boston's schools. Throughout the North, white children and free black children attended separate schools.

In 1851, Sumner was elected to the U.S. Senate from Massachusetts. He was among the strongest supporters of abolition, and he wrote, "Prejudice is the child of ignorance. It is sure to prevail, where people do not know each other." In 1856, after Sumner spoke out against slavery and allegedly insulted the uncle of Congressman Preston Brooks of South Carolina, Brooks physically attacked Sumner so violently that Sumner was forced to leave the Senate for three years.

After Abraham Lincoln's death, Sumner opposed President Johnson's Reconstruction plan. Sumner remained one of the strongest supporters of equal rights for African Americans until his death in 1874.

Charles Sumner was an abolitionist and a leader of the Radical Republicans.

CONFLICT BETWEEN PRESIDENT AND CONGRESS

The moderate Republicans were furious at President Johnson for vetoing the civil rights bill, so they came up with another solution. They passed the Fourteenth Amendment of the Constitution. President Johnson could not veto the amendment if it was approved by a majority of the states. The Fourteenth Amendment guaranteed equal rights for every citizen. However, it mentioned nothing about voting rights. Republicans wanted Southern states to agree to support the amendment before they could be readmitted to the Union.

Meanwhile, violence broke out in the South. On May 1, 1866, a conflict began between whites and blacks in Memphis, Tennessee. This was President Johnson's home state. The conflict started after a collision between a white carriage driver and a black driver. Police blamed the black driver. Crowds of whites and blacks began to gather, and a riot erupted.

Over the next three days, white mobs led by the police attacked many blacks. According to a report by the Freedmen's Bureau, the whites were inflamed when a city official, John C. Creighton, "in a speech which received three hearty cheers from the crowd there assembled . . . urged the whites to arm and kill every Negro and drive the

Thaddeus Stevens said that "every man, no matter what his race or color; every earthly being who has an immortal soul, has an equal right to justice, honesty, and fair play with every other man; and the law should secure him those rights."

last one from the city." Forty-six African Americans were killed. The report said that "they were shot down without mercy, women suffered alike with the men, and in several instances little children were killed. . . . One woman (Rachel Johnson) was shot and then thrown into the flames of a burning house." Black churches, school buildings, and 50 homes were destroyed.

In this cartoon from 1866, President Andrew Johnson holds a leaking kettle labeled "The Reconstructed South" toward a woman representing liberty who is carrying a baby representing the newly approved Fourteenth Amendment to the Constitution.

RIOT IN NEW ORLEANS

Almost three months after the Memphis riot, on July 30, 1866, another riot broke out in New Orleans when a group of African Americans were on their way to a nearby convention. The delegates to the convention were going to talk about taking voting rights away from former Confederate soldiers and giving the vote to former slaves. As the African Americans tried to get to the convention hall, they ran into a large group of whites. Conflict began, and 37 men—mostly African Americans—were killed. Former vice president Hannibal Hamlin (who had served during Abraham Lincoln's first term) said, "The wholesale slaughter and the little regard paid to human life I witnessed here" were worse than anything he had seen during the Civil War. Another observer added, "It was no riot; it was an absolute massacre."

More riots occurred in other towns and cities across the South, including Vicksburg, Mississippi; Eutaw, Alabama; Camilla, Georgia; and Hamburg, South Carolina. In Camilla, nine African Americans were killed and possibly as many as 40 were wounded. Historian James G. Hollandsworth Jr. has pointed out that the riots had a major impact on the course of Reconstruction. In August 1866, President Johnson went on a national tour to gain support for his Reconstruction plan. He urged white Southerners not to support the Fourteenth Amendment. However, the riots swayed voters in the other direction. Northern voters became convinced that Johnson's plan was not working. Instead of supporting Johnson, they elected representatives who supported the civil rights bill and the Fourteenth Amendment.

A RADICAL RECONSTRUCTION PLAN

In the South, the new state governments refused to approve the Fourteenth Amendment. This set up a conflict with the Republicans who controlled Congress. Most Republicans did not trust the new governments in the Southern states. Republicans thought that these states prevented African Americans from enjoying equal rights.

Early in 1867, the Republicans passed a new, harsh Reconstruction Act. According to this act, the Southern states were divided into five military districts. Each area was run by a U.S. Army commander. Troops were also stationed in each district to make sure that federal laws were enforced.

The Reconstruction Act of 1867 required Southern states to develop new state constitutions that supported the Fourteenth Amendment. Most important, African-American men were given the right to vote. Confederate leaders, however, were not permitted to vote in elections.

After almost 250 years of slavery, African Americans now found themselves with political power. "The only salvation for us besides the power of the Government," one former slave said, "is in the *possession of the ballot.* Give us this, and we will protect ourselves." With the power to vote, African-American men hoped that they could help make new laws in Southern states. These new laws would protect them against the power of whites who were prejudiced against them. A group of African Americans in Alabama said, "We claim *the same rights . . . as are enjoyed by white men.* We asked nothing more and will be content with nothing less. The law no longer knows white nor black, but simply men."

4

A New Political Role

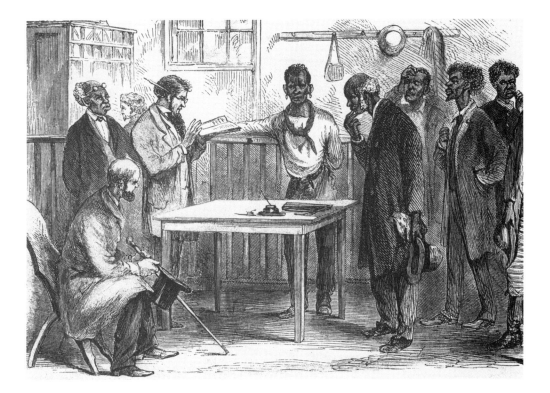

This 1867 engraving shows freed blacks in a voter registration office in Macon, Georgia. In the fall of that year, voters in the South elected delegates to constitutional conventions. More than a quarter of the elected delegates were black.

THE UNION LEAGUE

Since African Americans had received the vote, they wanted to learn about political issues. Many of them joined Union League clubs. The Union League was founded in Pennsylvania during the Civil War to support the Northern war effort. After the war, Union League clubs were formed in the South by the Republican Party to persuade members to support Republicans. Recruiters traveled around the South, trying to interest African Americans in becoming Union League members and setting up new clubs. Some of the recruiters came from the North. Others were members of the Freedmen's Bureau, and a few were African Americans from the South.

Among the recruiters was the Reverend James D. Lynch. As Lynch put it, "I commence as a preacher and end as a political speaker." Lynch's work took him to Mississippi. He spoke at large meetings of African Americans and helped them establish Union League clubs. Lynch helped form clubs in Vicksburg and Jackson, Mississippi. Many Southern whites were opposed to the Union League because it supported the Republican Party and equal rights for African Americans. Some Union League organizers had even been murdered by angry whites. To protect themselves, Union League members formed militia units. These units safeguarded African Americans when they voted for Republican candidates or ran for public office themselves.

African Americans in the South were strong supporters of the Republican Party after the Civil War. They felt grateful to Abraham Lincoln and the Republicans for the Emancipation Proclamation, the Thirteenth and Fourteenth

Amendments, and the Reconstruction Act of 1867. They also believed that Republicans would help blacks play a strong role in politics during the decades ahead.

CARPETBAGGERS AND SCALAWAGS

Along with the blacks who joined the Republican Party, the party also had white supporters in the South. Some were whites who had come from the North. White Southerners called them *carpetbaggers.* This was a term of disrespect referring to a carpetbag, or suitcase, that Northerners supposedly used

This cartoon from 1872 reflects the Southern view of Northern politicians as carpetbaggers. Northerners often criticized white Southerners' treatment of blacks during Reconstruction.

to travel lightly and quickly to the South. According to white Southerners, carpetbaggers had arrived to take advantage of the South and to get rich quick.

Some carpetbaggers did come south to buy up cotton plantations at low prices, but many others were successful Northern lawyers, teachers, and newspaper editors. Some also worked for the Freedmen's Bureau. Many of the carpetbaggers believed in the cause of achieving equal rights for

African Americans. A few even supported the demand of black farmers to obtain their own land. Many carpetbaggers also saw an opportunity to take control of the Republican Party in the South. By supporting equal rights for blacks, they could ensure the support of African Americans. With a large number of former slaves voting for Republicans, the party could win power in states throughout the South. This would enable Republicans to control Southern governorships and state legislatures. In addition, Republicans could elect many members to Congress and even the White House.

In addition to the carpetbaggers, another group of whites also supported the Republicans. These were Southern whites called *scalawags* by many Southerners. *Scalawag* was a term of disrespect that meant "scamp" or "rascal." Scalawags were considered traitors by other Southern whites for supporting African Americans and the Republican Party. However, the scalawags saw an opportunity to change politics in the South. Some were small farmers. Before the Civil War, they had had little power in Southern politics because political power had been controlled by wealthy cotton planters.

Some scalawags had opposed the South's seceding from the Union, although they fought for the South in the Civil War. While scalawags supported equal rights for African Americans, they did not want to put an end to segregation. As one of them said, "There is not the slightest reason why blacks and whites should sit in the same benches, in Churches, school houses, or Hotels. Each can have equal protection and benefits of the law without these."

James Lusk Alcorn

(1816–1894)

JAMES LUSK ALCORN was a leader of the scalawags in Mississippi. He was born in Illinois in 1816. After graduating from Cumberland College in Kentucky, Alcorn moved to Mississippi, where he became a successful lawyer.

Alcorn did not support Mississippi when it seceded from the Union. However, out of loyalty to the South, he joined the Confederate army. After the war, he supported equal rights for African Americans. Alcorn believed that by allying with African Americans, Southern whites might take control

Senator James Lusk Alcorn of Mississippi supported African-American rights following the Civil War.

of Reconstruction in the South. Alcorn said that he intended to "vote with the negro, discuss politics with him . . . and form a platform acceptable to both [races], and pluck our common liberty and prosperity from the jaws of inevitable ruin."

Alcorn was elected governor of Mississippi in 1869. Alcorn State University in Mississippi is named after him.

THE CONSTITUTIONAL CONVENTIONS

During the fall of 1867, voters in the South elected delegates to constitutional conventions. Many white Southerners refused to participate. They were primarily Democrats. They did not support the Reconstruction Act of 1867. As a result, most of the delegates were Republicans.

Out of a total of 1,000 delegates at the conventions, about one-sixth were carpetbaggers. The majority of delegates were scalawags, and 265 were African Americans. In Louisiana and South Carolina, blacks were a majority of the delegates. But in most states, they made up only 10 to 20 percent of the members of the conventions. More than 80 of the black delegates had been slaves before the Civil War. Other African Americans came from the North. Still others were free blacks living in the South. Many were clergymen, farmers, and teachers.

The constitutional conventions safeguarded equal rights for African Americans throughout the South. They also approved the Fourteenth Amendment and the right of black males to vote. On the other hand, they denied many former Confederates the right to vote.

Among the most important accomplishments of the constitutional conventions was setting up a system of public schools for whites and blacks. This program was very important to black delegates. It meant that their children could receive an education. However, the conventions made no effort to require that whites and blacks attend the same schools. Segregation remained the norm throughout the South.

African Americans wanted to buy or rent their own land, but white planters did not favor renting land to African Americans. Whites favored the gang system. Under this system, groups of African-American laborers, called *gangs,* worked the plantations and were paid in cash or with a share of the crop. However, African Americans did not like this system. It was too much like slavery, when gangs had been run by white overseers (supervisors). These overseers continued to direct the gangs on the plantations after the end of the Civil War. In addition, the gang system rewarded all workers equally, whether or not they had done an equal share of the work.

Eventually, whites and African Americans reached a compromise, called *sharecropping.* African-American families worked plots of land which were owned by the plantation owners. In return, the black families received a share of the crop that they harvested. This might be as much as one-third to one-half of the crop. The bigger the crop, the more the sharecroppers received. Sharecropping became widespread throughout the South during Reconstruction. While it was better than slavery, nevertheless, most African Americans were denied the opportunity to own any of their own land.

THE EDUCATION SYSTEM

Many historians believe that the most significant achievement of the entire Reconstruction era was setting up a broad public school system in the South. The education system was supported by money from state taxes. No such system devoted to educating white and black children had existed before 1867.

This engraving from 1866 shows black women being trained to make clothing at the Freedman's Union Industrial School in Richmond, Virginia.

Over the next decade, more and more children in the South attended school. By the early 1870s, most children in Texas were going to school. About 50 percent of white and black children in Mississippi, Florida, and South Carolina were in the classrooms.

African Americans recognized the importance of education. Unless they could read, blacks could not understand the voting ballots. As a result, they might be tricked by white Southerners into voting for the wrong candidates. African-American sharecroppers also signed contracts with white plantation owners. These contracts spelled out the size of the crops that the black farmers received. One black woman said she wanted to read "so that the Rebs ["rebels," or Confederates] can't cheat me."

Not only young people but adults went to schools to get an education. One observer noted that "six years and sixty may be seen side by side, learning to read from the same chart or book." Some classes were very large, with as many as 100 students. But African Americans did not care that the classrooms were crowded because they wanted to learn to read. Many children walked several miles to attend school. A member of the Freedmen's Bureau recalled, "At daylight in Winter, many of the pupils in the sparsely populated country places leave their home breakfastless for the school-house, five, six, or seven miles away." One teacher added that she had a student who walked miles to school every day and then went home and "taught his mother and two sisters all he has learned as we went along."

While many schools were built by states and local communities, others were financed by donations from African Americans. Black churches also built many schools. The American Methodist Episcopal Church ran several thousand schools in the South. As one observer said, "The Church and its schools were supported entirely by its members."

EDUCATING TEACHERS

Many of the teachers in these schools were white men and women who came from the North. But African Americans also wanted black instructors for their children. These black teachers presented positive role models. In the past, African

Black universities were often short of money. Many students were poor and could not afford to pay much tuition. Fisk University, founded in 1867, almost closed its doors in 1871. At this time, a group of students formed the Jubilee Singers. The singing group included two quartets under the direction of George L. White. The quartets went on tour in the North, raising $20,000. They sang black spirituals to large audiences and even appeared at the White House. This was the first time that many people in the North had heard these songs. The money raised by the singers helped to save Fisk University from closing. Today, Fisk remains one of America's best-known universities.

Americans had always been dominated by whites. Having white teachers instruct black children promoted this idea of inferiority. The problem was how to educate African-American teachers.

One way to accomplish this task was to set up black colleges to educate African Americans. The money for these colleges came from charitable organizations in the North, the Freedmen's Bureau, and the efforts of blacks in the South. Many schools were sponsored by religious groups, such as the Baptists and the Congregational Church. Among the colleges that were set up by the Congregational Church was Fisk University in Nashville, Tennessee, established in 1865.

Other such colleges included Howard University in Washington, D.C., and Talladega College in Alabama, both established in 1867, as well as Tougaloo College in Mississippi, established in 1869. Some of these colleges, such as Tougaloo, trained black teachers, while others, such as Howard, also trained African-American doctors and lawyers.

VIOLENCE AND THE KU KLUX KLAN

Many white Southerners opposed education for African Americans. An education might enable blacks to compete with whites for jobs and political power. Some whites burned down black schools. In the late 1860s, for example, 37 schools were destroyed in Tennessee. In Savannah, Georgia, in 1866, a black teacher was killed, while a teacher in Alabama was murdered in 1868.

Much of the violence against black teachers and schools was led by armed bands of whites. Among the best known of these groups was the Ku Klux Klan. The Klan was organized in Pulaski, Tennessee, in 1866, by six Confederate soldiers. The words *Ku Klux Klan* come from the Greek word *kuklos,* meaning "band" or "ring." At first the Klan was nothing more than a social club. Then members began riding around the countryside wearing white sheets and cone-shaped white hoods over their heads and faces. Sheets also covered their horses. Gradually, the Klan grew as more local groups began to form. Each group was called a den. The chief of each den was known as a cyclops.

Because membership in the Klan was secret and the members covered their faces when they rode across the countryside, the Klan was often known as the Invisible Empire. The Klan was committed to keeping African Americans in an inferior position. It also wanted to prevent the success of new governments based on equal rights. Its weapons were fear and violence, including murder.

During the slavery era, slave patrols had ridden along the roadways, terrorizing African Americans. The Klan was similar to these earlier armed bands. Generally, the Klansmen rode at night. They broke into the homes of African Americans and took any guns they found. Like many other whites, Klan members feared that African Americans might use the guns to start a violent revolution in the South. Klan members attacked black teachers and black clergymen. They rode up to the houses of black farmers and ordered the families outside. Then the Klansmen, using branches from nearby trees, whipped the blacks who did not kneel before them. One African-American political leader in Alabama named Allan A. Williams was beaten by the Klan in 1868.

One African American, F. H. Brown, recalled how the Klan terrorized African Americans. "They kept Negroes from voting. They would whip them. They put up notices: 'No Niggers to come out to the polls tomorrow.'"

The Klan also tried to prevent African Americans from going to the polls in elections and lynched blacks they suspected of committing crimes. Some African Americans soon formed their own militia groups to fight the Klan. Some Klansmen were killed in violent clashes with these militia.

Because the Klan was opposed to Radical Reconstruction, its victims were not only African Americans, but also white Republicans, scalawags, and carpetbaggers. They attacked a white Republican state legislator, 65-year-old William Wyatt of Tennessee, and beat him almost to death. On March 31, 1868, Klansmen broke into the house of George Ashburn, a leading Georgia Republican, and murdered him. No one was ever convicted of Ashburn's murder.

NEW LEADERS IN WASHINGTON

Early in 1868, voters in Southern states approved the new constitutions. They also voted for new state legislators and U.S. representatives to Congress. In most cases, the nominees running for political office were not African Americans. Republicans at the constitutional conventions were afraid of offending whites across the South by supporting black candidates. Instead, most of the candidates were scalawags and carpetbaggers. Only in South Carolina and Louisiana were blacks selected to run for state offices.

When the new congressmen arrived in Washington, they found the national capital in the midst of a major crisis. President Johnson had continued to oppose the new Reconstruction plan passed by Congress. Senators were afraid that Johnson might remove officials who supported Radical Reconstruction. Therefore, in 1867, Congress passed the Tenure of Office Act. This prevented Johnson from firing any high-ranking government official who had been approved by the Senate. (Under the Constitution, the Senate had to approve the nominations of high-ranking officials such as the members of Johnson's cabinet.) In defiance of the Tenure of Office Act, Johnson fired Edwin Stanton, his secretary of war, because Stanton opposed the president's policies on Reconstruction. Johnson also tried to persuade Southerners not to support the Reconstruction Act.

Early in 1868, the House of Representatives voted to impeach President Johnson. Impeachment is the legal process used to remove an elected official accused of committing a crime. Johnson was charged with defying the Tenure of Office

Act and trying to stop the Reconstruction Act of 1867. Under the Constitution, Johnson was tried by the Senate. Senator Charles Sumner called Johnson's impeachment "one of the last great battles with slavery." He called Johnson a representative of "the tyrannical slave power. In him, it lives again."

The impeachment trial of President Andrew Johnson opens in the Senate Chambers in 1868 in this U.S. Senate Historical Society drawing. Johnson was impeached and tried in the Senate, but he was not removed from office.

Most senators agreed that President Johnson was guilty. However, if they removed him from office, the new president would be Senator Benjamin Wade of Ohio. Johnson had no vice president. Under the Constitution, the next man in line for president was the leader of the Senate (called the president pro tem), which was Wade. Many senators did not like Wade, who was considered an ultra-radical Republican. By a margin of one vote, the Senate decided not to remove President Johnson from office.

ULYSSES S. GRANT

President Johnson did not run for reelection in 1868. Instead, the Republicans nominated General Ulysses S. Grant, the Union hero of the Civil War. The Democrats nominated former New York governor Horatio Seymour. They hoped to win the White House by opposing the Radical Reconstruction program, making it the main issue of the campaign. The Democrats believed that this platform would give them Southern support and help elect Seymour president. Grant, on the other hand, promised to continue the Reconstruction policies.

In the South, the Klan and other groups supported the Democrats and tried to prevent African Americans from voting for Republican candidates. Klansmen did not hesitate to use violence. In New Orleans, for example, they killed 200 black plantation workers. The Klan also terrorized black voters in Florida. To stop the Klan, the state government tried to bring in more rifles and ammunition for the state militia. A trainload of weapons made its way southward from New York. The local Klan heard that the train was approaching from Klan members who were telegraph operators working for the railroad. As the train entered Florida, the Klansmen jumped onto the cars. They broke open boxes of rifles and ammunition and threw them off the train. Then the Klansmen went back and destroyed them.

Many African Americans did not vote during the election of 1868. In Louisiana, for example, African Americans faced threats and violence from the Klan and from another organization called the Knights of the White Camellia. About 1,000 African Americans were killed in the months before the election. Some African Americans were so frightened that they voted for Democrats. Nevertheless, thousands of other African Americans went to the polls and voted Republican. General Grant was elected president, and Radical Reconstruction continued across the South.

5

Radical Reconstruction

This lithograph from 1872 is titled *The First Colored Senators and Representatives in the 41st and 42nd Congress of the United States.* Pictured in the top row are Robert C. DeLarge and Jefferson H. Long. In the bottom row are Hiram R. Revels, Benjamin S. Turner, Josiah T. Walls, Joseph H. Rainy, and R. Brown Elliot.

PROMINENT BLACK OFFICIALS

During Reconstruction, many African Americans were elected to political office. Most served at the state and local level. A few became members of the U.S. Congress. Black Republican politicians were often threatened by the Ku Klux Klan and other white groups. Despite the threat of violence, Republicans managed to improve state government, expand education programs, and provide more services to the poor.

States with Black Congressmen during Reconstruction

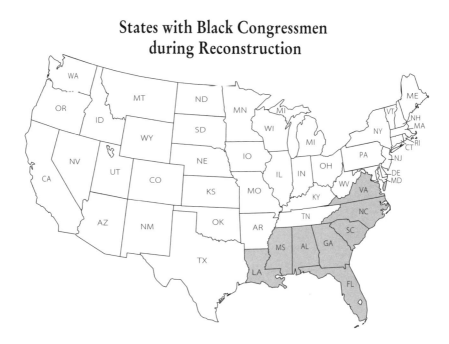

During Reconstruction, the former slave states of Alabama, Florida, Georgia, Louisiana, Mississippi, North Carolina, South Carolina, and Virginia all elected black representatives to Congress.

In only a few years, African Americans in the South moved from slavery to political office. Many African-American political leaders in the South during Reconstruction were ministers. These men were well educated and often very effective speakers—two important qualities for elected office. However, relatively few reached high office. Black Republican politicians were expected to take second place to white Republicans. Only 16 African Americans served in the U.S. Congress during the Reconstruction era. Among these men were Hiram R. Revels and Blanche Kelso Bruce, who were both elected to the U.S. Senate from Mississippi.

Revels was a free African-American minister who helped raise black units to fight for the Union during the Civil War. After the war, he became a religious leader in Mississippi. In 1870, he became the first black elected to the U.S. Senate. He served only a year because he was finishing out a Senate term that had been vacated during the war.

Blanche Bruce was born a slave in Virginia. He escaped in Missouri at the beginning of the Civil War. During the war, Bruce began the first school for African-American children in Missouri. Later, he became a landowner and an active member of the Republican Party in Mississippi and was elected to the U.S. Senate in 1874. He was the first African American to complete a full term (six years) in the Senate.

In addition to Bruce and Revels in the Senate, 14 African Americans were elected to the U.S. House of Representatives. John Willis Menard of Louisiana was the first African American elected to Congress. He was elected to the House in 1868. Eight of the other African Americans who served in the House came from South Carolina. Among the longest serving

After serving as a captain in the Union army during the Civil War, P. B. S. Pinchback was appointed lieutenant governor of Louisiana in 1871. When Governor Henry Clay Warmoth was impeached in 1872, Pinchback became acting governor. He was the only African-American governor until the late 20th century.

African-American congressmen was Robert Smalls. He served South Carolina in the House of Representatives from 1875 to 1886. Smalls was born a slave in Beaufort, South Carolina, in 1839. During the Civil War, he became a sailor on a Confederate merchant ship in Charleston. With the help of the other African Americans on board, Smalls took control of the ship and escaped to freedom. During the war, Smalls served in the Union navy and was wounded during a battle at Fort Sumter, South Carolina, in 1863. In 1870, Smalls was elected to the South Carolina state senate and afterward served five terms in Congress.

AFRICAN AMERICANS IN STATE GOVERNMENT

During Reconstruction, approximately 600 African Americans were elected to positions as state legislators. In South Carolina, there were enough African Americans in the legislature to form the majority. Indeed, 87 out of 127 of the state representatives in the late 1860s were newly elected black politicians. In other states, however, African Americans never made up a majority of the Republican political leaders. Most

Republicans were scalawags and carpetbaggers. They ran important committees in the state legislatures that developed the new laws for each state. A few African Americans, however, did achieve important positions such as secretary of the state and lieutenant governor. Alonzo Ransier served as lieutenant governor of South Carolina in 1870. One African American, P. B. S. Pinchback, served as lieutenant governor in Louisiana and later became governor when the white governor was impeached.

The Camilla Riot

Whether white or black, Republicans who were running for Congress often risked violence from white Southerners. In August 1868, Republicans in southern Georgia selected William P. Pierce, a white man, as their candidate for Congress. Pierce was a planter and an employee of the Freedmen's Bureau. He was supported by many African-American voters.

On September 19, Pierce and his black supporters planned an election rally in Camilla, Georgia. About 300 black supporters, including women and children, began a march toward Camilla, accompanied by a band. However, the white citizens of Camilla feared that the African Americans were a "mob" who meant to take control of the town. The whites fired on the procession as it entered Camilla. Some of the African Americans had brought guns and began shooting back, but they were quickly overwhelmed. The marchers fled to the woods, chased by whites. Nine African Americans were killed, and others were wounded. When it came time to vote for a congressman, very few Republicans dared to go to the polls in Camilla. Pierce lost the election.

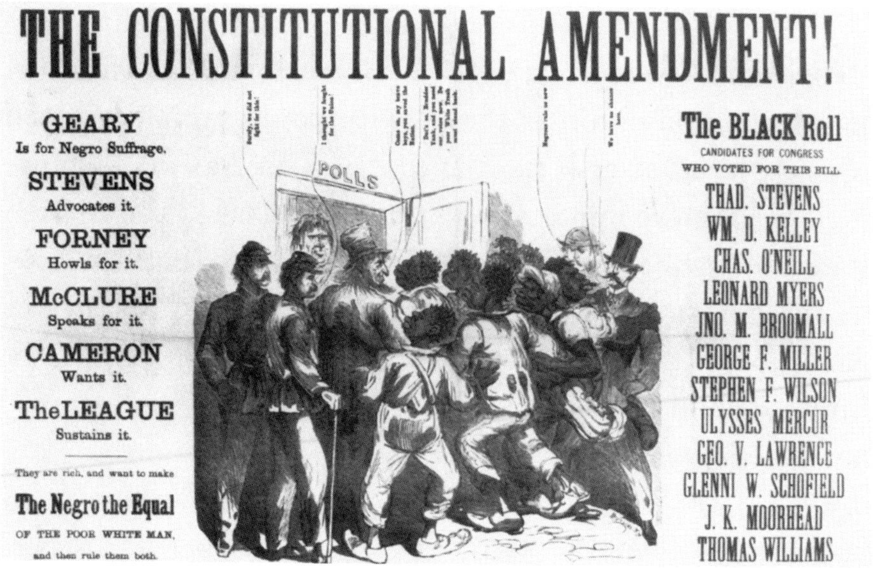
THE CONSTITUTIONAL AMENDMENT!
GEARY
Is for Negro Suffrage.
STEVENS
Advocates it.
FORNEY
Howls for it.
McCLURE
Speaks for it.
CAMERON
Wants it.
TheLEAGUE
Sustains it.
They are rich, and want to make
The Negro the Equal
OF THE POOR WHITE MAN,
and then rule them both.
POLLS
The BLACK Roll
CANDIDATES FOR CONGRESS
WHO VOTED FOR THIS BILL.
THAD. STEVENS
WM. D. KELLEY
CHAS. O'NEILL
LEONARD MYERS
JNO. M. BROOMALL
GEORGE F. MILLER
STEPHEN F. WILSON
ULYSSES MERCUR
GEO. V. LAWRENCE
GLENNI W. SCHOFIELD
J. K. MOORHEAD
THOMAS WILLIAMS

A highly racist poster from 1866 attacks postwar Republican efforts to pass a constitutional amendment giving blacks the right to vote.

The Republican governments in the South added many new state services. The most important was an extensive public school system. The system served black children, as well as whites. Among African Americans, only 14 percent could write before Reconstruction. By 1890, almost 50 percent of the black population could write English. In addition to schools, the state governments also built hospitals and orphanages. Some states also provided health care for poor people, many of them African Americans.

During Reconstruction, the South carried out a massive job of rebuilding the many cities that had been damaged or destroyed by Union attacks during the Civil War. State governments also built railroads in the South.

The large state programs in the South forced state governments to raise taxes. Many white planters complained about the higher taxes when they saw their tax dollars going to support schools and other facilities for African Americans.

Indeed, the Democratic Party used the tax issue to build support in the South. In some states, Democrats gradually came back into office during Reconstruction. A majority of whites supported Democratic candidates. In addition, some states gave back voting rights to former Confederates who had lost the right to vote during the early days of Reconstruction. In their election campaigns, Democrats said that they supported Radical Reconstruction. However, they criticized the high taxes and corruption in the Republican Party.

AFRICAN-AMERICAN OFFICIALS AT THE LOCAL LEVEL

More than 1,100 African-American officials served in local government during Reconstruction. They served as mayors, sheriffs, county treasurers, and judges. During the late 1860s, for example, African Americans served as sheriff, deputy sheriff, and justice of the peace in McIntosh County, Georgia. African Americans also served on juries, became police officers, and ran local jails. As a result, African Americans often found that they were treated far more fairly by the law than in former times.

The right of blacks to vote had brought an enormous change to the South. In 1869, Congress passed the Fifteenth Amendment to the Constitution. It gave every male adult citizen the right to vote, regardless of race, color, or whether they had once been slaves. The amendment was ratified by the states a year later. However, the Fifteenth Amendment did not eliminate all the problems facing black voters in the South. There were no secret ballots during the Reconstruction era. Therefore, whites at polling stations could see how African Americans voted. Whites who found black voters supporting the Republican Party might threaten them with violence. White landlords threatened black sharecroppers with loss of their land if they voted for Republicans.

Many whites believed that African Americans did not have the ability to vote intelligently. A group of whites in South Carolina compared African-American voters to white voters this way:

> *Intelligence, virtue, and patriotism are to give place, in all elections, to ignorance, stupidity and vice. . . . Those who own no property are to levy taxes and make all [spending decisions] . . . to support free schools for the education of the negro children, for the support of old negroes in the poor-houses, and the vicious in jails. . . . Every man's property will have to be sold to pay his taxes.*

Black voters who went alone to the polling stations often found themselves being threatened by white voters. In Barbour County, Alabama, Henry Frazer, a Republican organizer, never voted alone. He was accompanied by "450 men and camped at the side of the road." The men went together to the polling station and would "stand in a body until they got a chance to vote." Some polling stations were located far from

Elizabeth Van Lew

(1818–1900)

During the Civil War, ELIZABETH VAN LEW, a prominent resident of Richmond, did not support secession. She was in a small minority of white Southerners who believed in the Union. Defying public opinion, she visited Union prisoners in Richmond and brought them food. She even helped some of them escape. In 1864, as General Grant directed Union forces against Richmond, Van Lew ran a spy ring that provided Grant with intelligence about Confederate defenses.

Elizabeth Van Lew was a Union spy during the Civil War.

After the war, Van Lew was critical of the Reconstruction policy of President Johnson. She thought it was too lenient to former Confederate leaders and gave too little to former slaves. Following Grant's election as president in 1868, she was appointed postmaster of Richmond. At that time, only 1 percent of American postmasters were females. Van Lew promptly began hiring African Americans as letter carriers and clerks.

African-American farms, so black voters had trouble reaching them. At some polling stations, black voters were told they had to prove their ability to read before being allowed to vote. In other areas, they were forced to pay a tax—called a poll tax—which few African Americans could afford.

African Americans in the North

The passage of the Fifteenth Amendment guaranteed the right to vote for African-American men. Before its passage, many Northern states had barred black citizens from voting and passed strict segregation laws. During the 1860s, however, some states began passing laws against segregation. In 1867, Philadelphia, Pennsylvania, ended segregation on streetcars. In 1873, New York lawmakers prohibited segregation in public places, like theaters and parks. Some cities, including Chicago, Illinois, and Cleveland, Ohio, integrated public schools—that is, white and African-American children were permitted to attend the same schools. Connecticut and Rhode Island also passed laws supporting integration. But in many other areas in the North, school segregation continued.

INCREASED VIOLENCE BY THE KLAN

Meanwhile, violence continued across the South. White-sheeted members of the Ku Klux Klan rode across the South, trying to stop Reconstruction. Republican leaders were driven out of their counties. The Klan also attacked any African Americans suspected of crimes. In December 1868, Klansmen tortured Caswell Holt of North Carolina, suspecting he was a thief. Many Klan members took off their masks, and Holt saw their faces. He took the Klan members to court, but a judge would not convict them because Holt did not have any witnesses. After the trial, the Klan attacked Holt's home and fatally shot him.

This engraving shows two members of the Ku Klux Klan who were captured in Huntsville, Alabama, at a riot in 1868 in their robes and hoods.

The Klan and Robert Flournoy

In one Mississippi county, the Klan decided to attack the superintendent of schools, Robert Flournoy. He was a Civil War veteran who had fought in the Confederate army, but he strongly believed in educating African-American students. His views upset the Klan, but Flournoy would not back down. When a group of Klansmen arrived near Flournoy's home on May 12, 1871, he was ready for them. Flournoy and some of his friends armed themselves and met the Klan in the street. They asked the Klansmen to stop their campaign of violence against Flournoy. Instead, the Klan started shooting, and Flournoy's men shot back. One of the Klansmen was killed while the others ran. They never bothered Flournoy again.

African-American share-croppers were often driven from their land just before they were supposed to be paid for their work. This some-times occurred about the time when elections were held. In the fall of 1870, several counties in South Carolina became the scene of terrible violence. At least 11 African Americans were killed and hundreds whipped for voting for Republicans in congres-sional elections.

In Alamance County, North Carolina, Klansmen took several African Americans from the local jail in July 1869. The blacks were suspected of setting barns on fire. The Klan lynched the men without a trial, then did the same to some of their relatives. On one of the bodies was a note: "All barn-burners . . . we Kuklux hang by the neck till they are dead, dead, dead." That same year, a disabled schoolteacher named Alonzo Corliss was taken from his house and whipped repeatedly. One side of his head was painted black by the Klansmen.

Republican governor William Holden of North Carolina tried to stop the Klan. He sent in the state militia and arrested many Klansmen, who were discovered to be farmers, lawyers, and a few local sheriffs. The Klan was temporarily stopped in some parts of North Carolina. But no witnesses came forward to give evidence against the Klansmen, who were later released. Many people did not support what Holden had done. As a result, Democrats were elected to the state legislature in 1870. Some of them were members of the Klan. The legislature voted to impeach Holden. He was removed as governor early in 1871.

Klan violence and threats of violence occurred in other states, as well. Klansmen operated in Georgia, Mississippi, and Alabama. There were many violent incidents there in 1869 and 1870. Alabama passed laws prohibiting people from burning churches or schools and riding around in masks and other disguises, but these laws were never enforced against the Klan. The Klansmen attacked white Republicans and black political leaders. During a three-month period in 1870, seven Republicans were murdered. The Klan also destroyed black schools, forcing their teachers to leave.

THE KU KLUX KLAN ACT

By this time, the U.S. Congress had begun to act against the Ku Klux Klan. In the past, the violence committed by the Klan was a crime against state laws. In 1870, Congress passed the Enforcement Act. This now made it a federal crime for groups wearing disguises to prevent any Americans from exercising their equal rights, like voting. At first, little was done to enforce this law. As a result, Klan violence continued. Many voters were outraged by what the Klan was doing. They demanded that their congressional representatives do more to stop the Klan.

In 1871, Congress passed the Ku Klux Klan Act. Heavy fines now had to be paid by anyone violating an individual's civil rights. In addition, the act gave the president of the United States the power to use the army to stop the Klan.

After the Ku Klux Klan Act was passed, President Grant directed detectives to travel to the South secretly in order to find out as much as possible about Klan members. With this evidence, federal prosecutors brought several hundred Klansmen to trial. The prosecutors received help from federal troops. Trials were held in various states, including Georgia, Mississippi, and the Carolinas. Many Klansmen were found guilty. Others fled from the states where they lived.

Congress set up a committee to investigate the Klan. The committee held meetings in the South. Some people came forward to give evidence against the Klan, but many others were too scared to appear. Nevertheless, the Ku Klux Klan Act helped stop Klan activity throughout the South. By this time, however, many African Americans were too afraid to vote. In addition, many Republican leaders had been driven out of office by the Klan. Across the South, Democrats were taking back control.

6

The End of Reconstruction

In this cartoon from 1877, following the withdrawal of federal troops
from the South and the end of Reconstruction, President Hayes
conducts a carpetbagger to a train heading to the North.

TROUBLE IN LOUISIANA

In 1872, President Grant was reelected to a second term in office. He promised to continue protecting African Americans in the South. After Grant's reelection, the Reconstruction era entered its final period—from 1873 to 1877. African Americans tried to achieve greater political power in the South. However, they faced opposition from many whites. As a result, violence broke out in various Southern states. Meanwhile, Northerners had largely lost interest in Reconstruction. Instead, they were concerned about a terrible economic depression that affected the entire country. When a new American president was elected in 1876, he soon brought an end to Reconstruction.

President Grant said he would prevent violence in the South. This 1874 cartoon shows Grant going against the White League, which briefly took control of New Orleans, Louisiana, in September of that year until Grant sent federal troops to the city.

In 1873, a close election for governor occurred in Louisiana. The Democratic candidate was supported by some white Republicans who believed that African Americans were achieving too much power. When President Grant declared the Republican candidate the winner, Democrats refused to listen. They tried to take control of New Orleans. Federal troops and the local police finally enabled Republicans to stay in power.

Many Republicans in Louisiana feared that Democrats might try to take control of local governments. In Colfax, Louisiana, a unit of the state militia made up of Republican African Americans took over the courthouse. At the same time, a large group of armed white vigilantes gathered outside of Colfax. On April 7, 1873, the white vigilantes arrived in town. On April 13, they brought in a cannon and began shooting at the courthouse. The militia began to retreat. Forty of the black militiamen were captured by the vigilantes and shot to death.

Death in Colfax

Colfax is located on the Red River, about 200 miles (320 km) from New Orleans. Today, a historic marker stands in front of the courthouse. It states: "On this site occurred the Colfax Riot in which three white men and 150 negroes were slain. This event on April 13, 1873, marked the end of carpetbag misrule in the South." The marker is not entirely accurate. Reconstruction did not end in 1873—but attitudes toward it were changing, especially in the North. Among the whites killed at Colfax were James Hadnot and Sidney Harris. In the local cemetery at Colfax is a marble plaque. It reads: "In loving remembrance erected to the memory of the heroes . . . James West Hadnot [and] Sidney Harris who fell in the Colfax Riot fighting for white supremacy."

After Colfax, white vigilante groups continued to form in Louisiana, as well as in Mississippi. They called themselves the White League. Many had been members of the Ku Klux Klan or the Knights of the White Camellia. In September 1874, 9,000 members of the White League invaded New Orleans to take it over from the Republicans. Local police and the state militia could not stop the league. At this point, President Grant sent federal troops to New Orleans, and they forced the White League out of the city.

A cartoon from a Northern newspaper of 1874 shows members of the White League in Louisiana trying to intimidate and disenfranchise black voters.

THE NATIONAL DEPRESSION

Many Northerners were very upset by the violence in the South. They began to believe that Reconstruction might have gone too far. In addition, Northerners thought that the cost of Reconstruction and maintaining troops in the South was too expensive.

On October 1, the large banking firm of Jay Cooke & Company declared bankruptcy. Smaller banks were immediately affected because they had invested with Jay Cooke. These banks in turn had loaned money to many merchants, farmers, and factory owners. The banks asked for these loans to be paid, but the borrowers did not have the money. So the borrowers went bankrupt and laid off thousands of workers.

By the end of 1873, the United States had entered a deep economic depression. In New York City, the unemployment rate reached 25 percent. The unemployed asked for help from local governments, but the governments had no money to give laid-off workers. Those who continued to work often saw their wages cut as employers tried to reduce expenses. Massive strikes broke out at factories and mines. These frightened many people throughout the North. They feared that workers might try to take control of businesses. The depression would continue through much of the 1870s.

The Panic of 1873 had an enormous impact in the South. The demand for cotton and tobacco fell. Many well-to-do white plantation owners and small African-American farmers went broke. Black farmers and artisans had put their money in the Freedman's Savings and Trust Company. In June 1874, the bank closed, and many African Americans lost all their savings. Republican state governments had committed themselves to providing more services for the poor, but the nationwide depression made these programs impossible.

Voters blamed Republicans for the national depression. In the congressional elections of 1874, people voted overwhelmingly for Democrats. They took control of Congress. The Democratic victory sent a signal to many white Southerners that Reconstruction might no longer receive support in Congress.

AFRICAN-AMERICAN POLITICAL LEADERS

The economic depression and the Democratic victory could not have come at a worse time for African-American politicians in the South. A conflict had been growing between white and black Republicans. Scalawags and carpetbaggers had filled most of the high political offices in the South during Reconstruction. These white Republicans believed that it was their role to lead and that African Americans should follow them. Lower offices in local government and a minority of seats in state legislatures had been left to African Americans. Black voters had grown tired of this situation. Refusing to back white Republican candidates any longer, they elected more African Americans. By the end of 1874, there were larger numbers of black officials serving in state legislatures in the South and in the U.S. Congress.

Northerners, however, were far more concerned with the economic depression than they were with Reconstruction. Strikes in the North made them afraid that poor and working-class people might be threatening the middle classes. Northerners saw a similar situation in the South, where poor African-American voters were electing their candidates to state legislatures. Well-to-do whites, on the other hand, had lost much of their power.

In this newspaper cartoon from 1877, President Ulysses S. Grant struggles beneath the burdens of corruption that beset his government. The hounds pursuing him represent the press.

In Hamburg, South Carolina, the local militia unit was led by a black man named Dock Adams. On July 4, 1876, Adams led a parade along the main street of the town. An argument broke out between Adams and two white men in a carriage. They wanted the parade to stop so they could cross the street. The problem was solved when Adams backed down.

Several days later, the white men came back to Hamburg with a group of armed supporters. Firing broke out between the whites and the black militia, led by Adams. Several African Americans were killed, including the local sheriff. Although Adams escaped, some of his men were captured. Five of these prisoners were then murdered by the white vigilantes. One of the vigilantes said, "We are going to start at Hamburg and we are going to clean out the government offices . . . to the last one in South Carolina."

An 1876 cartoon shows Samuel Tilden, the Democratic presidential nominee, disassociating himself from the Hamburg, South Carolina, massacre.

Corruption was another issue that troubled many Northerners. President Grant's administration had been struck by several major scandals. One involved officials in the Treasury Department. They had taken bribes from liquor manufacturers. Another scandal involved Secretary of War William Belknap. He was bribed by merchants who wanted government contracts to trade with American Indians. Many voters saw a similarity between the scandals in the Grant administration and the corruption in Republican state governments in the South. They believed that these practices might end if white Democrats returned to power.

THE PRESIDENTIAL ELECTION OF 1876

In 1876, Republicans nominated Rutherford B. Hayes for the presidency of the United States. Hayes had served as a major-general in the Union army during the Civil War. He was later elected congressman and governor of Ohio. The Democrats nominated Samuel Tilden, governor of New York.

On election day, the early returns showed that Tilden was winning, but as more returns came in, Hayes seemed to be pulling ahead. However, the election returns in three Southern states, Florida, South Carolina, and Louisiana, were still in doubt. Violence had occurred in these states during the presidential election. Local election officials said that some Democratic ballots were cast illegally. As a result, Hayes was declared president of the United States. Democrats protested that he had "stolen" the election.

At first, it appeared that Democrats would not accept Hayes as the legally elected president. However, Hayes

Samuel Tilden did not support Radical Reconstruction after the Civil War. Tilden was elected governor of New York in 1874 and was known primarily for exposing corrupt politicians in New York City.

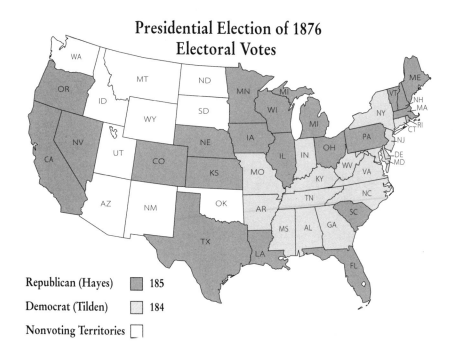

Presidential Election of 1876
Electoral Votes

Republican (Hayes) ▮ 185

Democrat (Tilden) ▯ 184

Nonvoting Territories ▢

Republican candidate Rutherford B. Hayes received only one more electoral vote than his opponent, Democrat Samuel Tilden, in the presidential election of 1876.

indicated that if he were elected president, federal troops would be withdrawn from the South. This pleased the Democrats. They did not try to stand in the way of the decision reached by the electoral commission. As a result, Hayes became the 19th president of the United States.

Without the support of federal troops, Republicans and African Americans could no longer remain in power in the South. Reconstruction was coming to a close.

7

The Impact of Reconstruction

A jury made up of both blacks and whites in a Southern courtroom during the Reconstruction era.

MOVING BACKWARD

Reconstruction ended in 1877. By this time, white Democrats had taken back control of state legislatures and governorships across the South. African Americans continued to vote and even elect public officials. However, black Americans gradually returned to an inferior position in the South. African-American educator and author W. E. B. DuBois wrote that "the slave went free; stood a brief moment in the sun; then moved back again toward slavery."

In 1877, President Hayes removed the last federal troops from the South. Southern Redeemers, as they called themselves, had taken power away from Republicans and African Americans. A newspaper in Richmond, Virginia, proclaimed that the "best Government in the world" was the "rule of the best people." According to the newspaper, this meant white, Democratic politicians, who "own the property. They have the intelligence. Theirs is the responsibility. For these reasons they are entitled to control. . . . They are the superior race, and will not and cannot submit to the domination of an inferior race."

In his inaugural address, President Hayes said of the Southern states that "the inestimable blessing of wise, honest, and peaceful local self-government is not fully enjoyed . . . only a local government which recognizes and maintains inviolate the rights of all is a true self-government."

Black voters did not stop going to the polls. In North Carolina, 52 African-American politicians sat in the state legislature between 1876 and 1894. Almost as many black legislators were elected in South Carolina during approximately the same time. In Virginia, a former slave, Henry D. Smith, was elected to the state legislature from Greensville County in 1879. John W. Poindexter, a free black man, became a state representative from Louisa County in 1875. About the same time, Ballard T. Edwards represented Chesterfield County and served as justice of the peace.

In some Southern states, whites made blacks take tests to prove they could read before allowing the blacks to vote. This cartoon from the 1870s makes fun of such tests.

Southern Democrats force a black voter to vote the Democratic ticket in this cartoon published in a magazine just before the presidential election of 1876.

Nevertheless, whites made every effort to control the way African Americans voted. Since many of them worked for white plantation owners, they had little choice but to obey. One white woman explained that her husband, a plantation owner, "got most of our tenants to vote right, or if not to stay at home and not vote at all." One black farmer, John Anderson, had disobeyed. Anderson, she said, "will not be on the place next year."

African Americans who did not listen to white landowners faced a difficult time in the South. Jack Turner had been a slave in Choctaw County, Alabama. During Reconstruction, he purchased a small piece of land and became a farmer. A big man who was respected in the black community, Turner also worked as a Republican organizer. Once Reconstruction ended, Turner continued to persuade black voters not to support the white plantation owners.

Turner was feared by whites in Choctaw County. Whites believed that he would lead a mob against them. In 1882, white officials arrested him. They accused Turner of plotting to kill every white person in the county. Before Turner could be tried, a white mob gathered outside the local jailhouse, dragged Turner from his cell, and lynched him.

Whites used many other methods than violence to stop African Americans from voting. As before, voting stations were placed far away so black farmers would have long distances to travel to vote. Some voting booths were mysteriously closed on Election Day. Votes were counted by white officials who always declared the white candidate the winner. Many areas also charged voters a poll tax which was too high for most African Americans to pay.

NEW STATE LAWS

With white Democrats back in power, government programs changed. Taxes were greatly reduced. Plantation owners were no longer taxed on all their property. State legislatures passed harsh laws against vagrants. Anyone who was not employed could be arrested. In addition, any employees who had a contract with a plantation owner were not permitted to leave until all their work was done. African Americans could not leave

When Southern universities invited white students to return after Reconstruction, white professors were also asked to come back. A white professor was told by a member of the university's governing board, "Nothing could be farther from my thoughts than suggesting . . . that you should return here to teach negroes, or to connect yourself with any educational institution in which they are present or are likely to be present in social or other equality with our race."

the plantations where they worked. Meanwhile, the courts were controlled by whites. After Reconstruction, African Americans were no longer permitted to sit on juries. Black sheriffs also disappeared.

Among the most important changes during Reconstruction was setting up a public school system for black and white children. Since the new state governments cut taxes, they no longer had as much money to support education. Black schools were especially hard hit. There was little money to pay teachers or buy supplies.

Students suffered at all levels of education. During Reconstruction, the University of South Carolina had begun admitting black students. White students and professors left the university in protest. James H. Johnson, a black student, entered the university in 1874. When Reconstruction ended his junior year, so did his college education. African Americans were forced out of the university, which invited whites to return.

Some colleges continued to accept African-American students. These included Alcorn State University in Mississippi. But in 1878, the name of the school was changed to Alcorn Agricultural and Mechanical College. Whites who ran the school believed that African Americans did not need a liberal arts education but should be taught only vocational skills so they could get jobs on farms or in industry. Hampton Institute in Virginia had been established to educate black students, but Hampton also emphasized job skills. Students were told that if they worked hard, they would be successful. However, they were also advised to stay out of politics, which was run by white men.

KEEPING THEIR PLACE

African Americans, even those who were college educated, were learning to "keep their place" in the new South. This meant that they should recognize the white race as superior and blacks as inferior. Blacks who were told to work hard soon realized that, no matter how hard they worked, they could only get so far. Whites controlled the land and the wealth in the South. Most African Americans remained poor.

The vast majority of African Americans continued working on the plantations. Some rented land, while others worked for wages, and still others were sharecroppers. Planters forced the small farmers to grow cotton or tobacco. As a result, the poor sharecroppers could grow little food. Instead, they bought food from local stores, which were owned by the plantation owners. The food was purchased on credit. Sharecroppers had to pay interest for this credit—often as high as 50 percent. They promised to pay the store owners part of their cotton crop when it was sold.

This was called settling time, when all accounts were settled, but the sharecroppers were often cheated. The plantation owners, who sold the cotton crop, lied to the sharecroppers about how much money they had received for selling the cotton. The plantation owners—who also owned the stores—also lied about how much they were owed for the food purchased on credit. As a result, the sharecroppers found themselves in constant debt.

No matter how hard sharecropper families worked, they seemed unable to improve their lives. Husbands, wives, and children often worked side by side in the fields. Women were also responsible for cooking, washing clothes, and cleaning the cabins. One woman said, "Plenty of times, I've been to bed at three and four o'clock and get up at five[,] the first one in the morning. Just with the lord's help, that's all." Rosina Hoard, another sharecropper, said, "I had my house work and de cookin' to do and to look after de chillun, but I'd go out and still pick . . . cotton." Despite their hard work, most African Americans were never able to afford to buy any land. In 1880, only 1 percent of the African Americans living in a large region of Georgia owned any property.

The words of one popular song succinctly stated the plight of African-American sharecroppers: "Well, it makes no difference / How you make out your time / White man sho' to bring a / Black man out behin'."

African Americans in Latin America faced discrimination after they had been freed from slavery. Emancipation did not change white attitudes. For three centuries, whites had considered African Americans an inferior race. After emancipation, whites still regarded themselves as superior.

In many areas of Latin America, the population of African Americans was small. In Mexico, Peru, Chile, and Argentina, they made up only about 1 percent of the population. African Americans were not hired to work in factories, where whites considered them poor employees. As a result, African Americans were forced to take low-paying, menial jobs as maids and janitors. They did not possess the education or the job skills of many new immigrants who came to Latin America from Europe. In Mexico, Peru, and Argentina, African Americans lived in rundown housing in poor sections of large cities. On the Caribbean islands,

however, the population of African Americans was much larger and more prosperous. Here they used their money to purchase large farms and run them. Some African Americans also entered business and politics.

Slave laborers work on a Caribbean plantation in this illustration published in 1667.

THE FAILURE OF RECONSTRUCTION

Reconstruction was an attempt to change the South. Republicans and African Americans tried to end more than two centuries of racism. This is the belief that one group of people is inferior to another based only on race. Unfortunately, racism could not be changed in the South. Whites continued to feel superior to blacks. When they took back control, whites made sure that blacks were put back into an inferior position. Whites believed that African Americans were created to work in the fields. One planter said, "The mule and the [black man], you know, was made the same day, and they're just suited to each other." Whites saw no reason why African Americans should try to rise above their station in life. A newspaper said, "The only condition under which the two races can co-exist peacefully is that in which the superior race shall control and the inferior race shall obey."

Northern armies could not stop the violence in the South. Members of the Ku Klux Klan and the White League spread terror among blacks in many Southern states. They attacked African-American Republican leaders. White terrorists went after any black farmers who seemed to be achieving success and making some money. They also drove out teachers who worked with black children. The Klan and the White League were afraid that if African Americans received education, they would no longer feel inferior to whites.

Some African Americans tried to escape conditions in the South by moving to other parts of the United States. After the Civil War, about 40,000 African Americans traveled on steamboats up the Mississippi River to St. Louis, Missouri, and then to Kansas. Many others wanted to go, but they were too poor to afford the boat trip. Some farmers who tried to leave with their families were stopped by white plantation owners, who wanted to keep the sharecroppers on the plantations.

During the Reconstruction era, African Americans had made some improvements in their lives. Black families were reunited after slavery. Some black children received an education and continued attending school even after Reconstruction ended. A few entered black colleges. African Americans also established churches across the South. Many of them became thriving centers, not only of religious worship, but also of education and charity in black communities. Finally, the passages of the Fourteenth and Fifteenth Amendments promised African Americans the same rights as other citizens.

In 1879, thousands of African Americans took part in the exodus to the dusty Kansas plains. As a result they were called "exodusters" by residents of Kansas.

Nevertheless, most African Americans spent the years after Reconstruction in poverty, and they remained in inferior positions throughout the South. They were frequently prevented from exercising the rights given to them by the U.S. Constitution. Instead, African Americans were the victims of racism. This situation would not change for almost another century.

Time Line

1860	More than 4 million African-American slaves live in the United States. Slavery has been abolished throughout most of Latin America. Abraham Lincoln is elected president.
1861	Southern states secede from the Union. The Civil War begins, dividing North from South for four years.
1862	President Lincoln declares that his object is to save the Union, not free the slaves. Congress passes the Militia Act, permitting the president to free slaves who join the Union cause.
1863	Confederate forces are defeated at Gettysburg and other battles; Union forces invade the South. President Lincoln issues the Emancipation Proclamation and develops the Ten Percent Plan.
1864	Union forces continue to succeed against the Confederacy. Lincoln is elected to his second term.
1865	The South surrenders, ending the Civil War. Lincoln is assassinated on April 14 by John Wilkes Booth, a Southern sympathizer. Andrew Johnson becomes president and proposes a new Reconstruction plan. The Freedmen's Bureau is established. The Thirteenth Amendment ending slavery in the United States is ratified. Universities and colleges intended to educate blacks begin to open throughout the South.

1866	The Southern states return to the Union and pass the Black Codes. The Ku Klux Klan is formed in Pulaski, Tennessee; it soon spreads to other Southern states. Race riots break out in New Orleans and Memphis.
1867	Republicans develop the Radical Reconstruction plan and pass the Reconstruction Act of 1867. The Southern states are divided into five military districts and occupied by Union troops. Southern states hold constitutional conventions. Thousands of former slaves vote in local and national elections.
1868	The Fourteenth Amendment guaranteeing equal rights for every U.S. citizen is ratified. President Johnson is impeached but not removed from office. African Americans are elected to state legislatures in the South. John W. Menard becomes the first African American elected to Congress. Ulysses S. Grant is elected president of the United States.
1869–1871	The Ku Klux Klan terrorizes African Americans in the South.
1870	Hiram R. Revels becomes the first African American elected to the U.S. Senate. The Ku Klux Klan murders seven Republican leaders in Alabama. Congress passes the Enforcement Act, making it a crime to prevent any American from exercising his or her civil rights.

1871	Congress passes the Ku Klux Klan Act, giving the president the power to use the army against the Klan. Most Klan activity is stopped.
1872	President Grant is reelected.
1873	The Colfax Riot occurs in Louisiana. The White League is formed. The economic Panic of 1873 begins; unemployment soars to 25 percent in New York City; cotton and tobacco prices fall sharply.
1874	New Orleans is invaded by 9,000 members of the White League. The Democrats take control of Congress and begin to end Reconstruction.
1876	The Hamburg Massacre occurs in South Carolina. Violence breaks out in South Carolina during the governor's race. Rutherford Hayes is elected president of the United States.
1877	Reconstruction ends. Federal troops are withdrawn from Southern states.

Glossary

carpetbaggers A term of disrespect used by Southerners to describe Northerners who went to the South to support the Republican Party after the Civil War; white Southerners believed that these Northerners had come to take advantage of the South.

civil rights The rights of personal liberty guaranteed by the U.S. Constitution.

emancipation The act of freeing slaves.

Fifteenth Amendment An amendment to the U.S. Constitution guaranteeing voting rights for all male citizens.

Fourteenth Amendment An amendment to the U.S. Constitution guaranteeing equal rights for African Americans.

Freedmen's Bureau An organization that assisted the newly freed African Americans after the Civil War.

Ku Klux Klan A white racist group that used violence against African Americans throughout the South.

lynch To murder by mob action, without a legal trial

plantation A large farm that relied on slaves to produce one main crop.

prejudice An unreasonable bias against or intolerance of others.

racism Prejudice based on race.

Reconstruction A federal program after the Civil War to readmit Southern states into the Union and provide equal rights for African Americans.

scalawags White Southerners who supported the Republican Party.

secede To break away from a larger group or government and become independent.

segregation Separating whites and blacks and requiring them to use different public facilities, such as parks and schools.

sharecropping A system in which a farmer worked on part of a plantation in return for a share of the crop.

spiritual A folk hymn of a type developed by blacks in the American South that combined African and European elements and expressed deep emotion.

Thirteenth Amendment An amendment to the U.S. Constitution prohibiting slavery.

Further Reading

BOOKS

Altman, Susan. *Extraordinary African-Americans.* New York: Children's Press, 2001.

Beckner, Chrisanne. *100 African-Americans Who Shaped American History.* San Francisco: Bluewood Books, 1995.

Cooper, Michael. *From Slave to Civil War Hero: The Life and Times of Robert Smalls.* New York: Lodestar Books, 1994.

Dudley, William, ed. *Reconstruction.* San Diego: Greenhaven Press, 2003.

Frankel, Noralee. *Break Those Chains at Last: African Americans, 1860–1880.* New York: Oxford University Press, 1996.

WEB SITES

Freedmen's Bureau Online. "Report of the 1866 Memphis, Tennessee, Riot." URL: http://freedmensbureau.com/tennessee/outrages/memphisriot.htm. Downloaded on May 6, 2005.

Hunter College Caribbean Studies. "African Americans in the Caribbean and Latin America." URL: http://www.saxakali.com/caribbean/shamil.htm. Downloaded on May 6, 2005.

Indiana University–Purdue University Indianapolis and the Southern Poverty Law Center. "The Ku Klux Klan: A Hundred Years of Terror." URL: http://www.iupui.edu/~aao/kkk.html. Downloaded on May 6, 2005.

Mississippi Historical Society. "Mississippi History Now: James Lusk Alcorn." URL: http://mshistory.k12.ms.us/features/feature47/governors/23_james_alcorn.htm. Downloaded on May 6, 2005.

Index

DATE DUE